Angels in the Wilderness

The True Story of One Woman's
Survival Against All Odds

By Amy Racina

www.AngelsInTheWilderness.com

Jan 10, 2007
To Bill &
Beth -
May you always
have happy
endings!

Amy Racina

Elite Books

Santa Rosa, CA 95403

www.Elitebooks.biz

Library of Congress Cataloging-in-Publication Data:

Racina, Amy. 1956-
    Angels in the wilderness : the true story of one woman's survival
against all odds / Any Racina. -- 1st ed.
    p. cm.
    ISBN 0-9710888-9-6

    1. Mountaineering accidents — Sierras, California.
    2. Self-actualization.   I. Title.
       2005

Interior design and cover by Nan Sea Love

Photos by Adrian Morgan and Art Bock

Typeset in Colonna and Hoefler Text

Printed in USA by Sheridan Books

First Edition

10 9 8 7 6 5 4 3 2 1

CONTENTS

To the angel in each of us,
and especially to my three wilderness angels
Jake, Leslie and Walter

ACKNOWLEDGMENTS

I dedicate this book to everyone who has ever made someone else's life a little brighter, especially to the angels in my own life. My most sincere personal thanks go to all the members of "HelpingAmy" and all who helped care for me in my time of need.

Thanks to Jake, Leslie, and Walter, my three wilderness angels, without whom the ending to my story would have been much different. Special thanks to my wilderness brother, Jake, for finding me, and to Walter for his heroic run out of the Tehipite.

I gratefully acknowledge Mark Johnson and the Reedley firefighters, and Debbie Brenchley, Fred Mason, and the National Park Service for their fine work, the CHP helicopter pilots for risking their own lives to save mine, and everyone else in the chain of rescue.

Sincere gratitude to all of the wonderful staff of University Medical Center in Fresno, and especially to Dr. Kenty Sian and Dr. Abraham Appleton, for doing such an expert job of putting me back together again.

To Diane, for being with me when I got out of surgery. To Sally, for watching over me in the hospital. To Francesca and Adrian and Carla and Sam and Daniel, for their visits and their advocacy at UMC.

Thanks to "Almira" for being my mirror. May some of the good you have done me reflect back upon you.

To the women from my women's circles; especially Dhyanis, Barb, Rebecca, Terrie, and Lorraine, for being my angels many times over; and to Deborah Boyar, for helping to spread the word.

To all the WaCCOs, the WaccoSingles, and the members of the North Bay Poly Community who took time off from their busy lives to help me restore my own. Thanks to Leela and Barry for the fund-raiser, to Linda for the never-ending potluck, to Miles for the "HelpingAmy" Web site, and to Francesca for coordinating.

To all who sent cards, flowers, books, magazines, and donations. To each person who offered good wishes, e-mails, prayers, and blessings. To the folks who brought food, donated equipment, offered up their time and effort and skills and expertise in my healing, recuperation, and the regaining of my life. To everyone who helped.

Thank you all for the prayers and gatherings and visionings from many spiritual traditions, the numerous thoughts and good wishes. They were all important.

To Amy's Kitchen, and to the many fine cooks who brought wonderful food.

Thanks to Dr. Thomas Miles, for taking my case, making me work like a junk yarddog, and being proud of me.

To my hero Eddie Rosen and his PTMEC therapists, Maria, Barbara, Mary, Lori, John, Sylvia. Thank you for the gift of walking. To Sonia, Carrie and Vita in the front office, for making my visits joyful, and making PT feel like home.

To the many drivers who helped me get to PT in those first crucial weeks; Edward, Sally, Carla, Adrian, Martha, Lauri, Lani, Glenneth, Clint, Big Sam, Kate, Leela, Francesca, Terrie, Barb, Dhyanis, Dan, and Kelly.

To the people at social services who guided me through the Medi-Cal process; special thanks to the eligibility worker who helped with that final miracle.

To Coleen and Lou for the purple ambulance, and the proofreading. To Sergio and Luisa for looking after my house. To Richard, for not being surprised that I survived. To Evan, for always making me feel beautiful.

To my Mom and Dad, for their many gifts in making me who I am, for their creative modeling, their inspiration, and their love. For teaching me not to give up.

To Jean and George Banning, for taking up where my parents left off, and taking on the difficult job of looking after me.

Grateful thanks for the ongoing support of my family, Dan, Kelly, Ellen, and especially my son Sam, for the inspirations as I watch him go through his own life.

Kudos to my women's writing group, Francesca, Mary, Lory O., and Molly, for teaching me to write from my heart. And to NaNoWriMo for showing me what it took to plunk down the words.

To Carla for remembering our promise, now and forever, and for always being there for me.

To Adrian, for his many acts of friendship, for all of the love, caring, support, and encouragement, the incentives of snowshoeing, ladder climbing and backpacking, for the many, many things he did to make my life brighter during the dark days of recovery.

To Francesca, for her encouragement, admiration, love, and friendship, for being the keeper of the archives, and for bringing her brilliant mind and an extraordinary heart to the editing process.

To Dawson Church, for believing in my book, my story, and in me.

1

The Fall

AUGUST 4, 2003

"So this is how it ends." The thought resounds through my shaken body. I have not blacked out: I remember the seconds of the free-fall with brutal clarity. I took a single step, just one more step in hundreds of thousands of steady paces along the trail. Suddenly, without warning, I was falling. I saw the harsh slab of rock rushing up toward me from sixty feet below. There was no bouncing, no sliding, no scrambling. No trees reached out their branches to offer me a handhold. No cushioning undergrowth slowed my plunge. There was no way to stop my descent, nothing to grab onto, no time to shift position, no action that could alter my fate as I plummeted through the air.

This was it. I was going to die. No gentle, easy passing into some brighter place. No life flashing gloriously before my eyes. No ecstatic freedom in my uncontrolled flight. Just this abrupt, thoughtless termination of life. I felt bitter disappointment at all that was lost to me. My mind screamed out in frustration against my own impotence, and my world went gray around me. I did not even have time to pray.

Months later it would come back to me, the sickening feeling of my own bones shattering as my body crashed like a rag doll upon the rock. But at the moment of impact, I felt nothing. Now I lie on my back on a slab of shale, legs crushed under me at an awkward angle, and look up at the wall of the ravine towering above me. The ominous wall is not a cliff, but rather a steep hillside. I recall the steps that led me to this impasse.

I'd been navigating that hillside, working my way cautiously around the circumference. Leery of heights and inclined to vertigo, I took care not to gaze down into the ravine. I focused instead on choosing a route that descended gradually around the hill. Scouting a few steps ahead with my eyes, I moved carefully. I had unclipped the waist belt of my backpack, as I often do, subtly shifting the weight and giving myself room to breathe without the compressing strap across my lower abdomen. I had been on the trail for two weeks already, and my pack was light—about twenty-one pounds. It felt like a part of me as I moved through the woods. I carried a single trekking pole in my right hand, using it for stability on the rocks and employing it as a probe to test a potentially risky ledge. I grabbed onto a large rock embedded in the hillside with my left hand and wrapped my right, still holding the slender hiking pole, around a scrawny tree, firmly rooted into the leaf covered ground. Only then did I reach out my right foot and allow my weight to sink gradually onto it. I focused on that single step, thinking longingly of the stable ground far below.

Sierra View—Kings-Kern Divide from Goat Mountain.
Photo by William L. Neelands.

In less than a heartbeat, I was betrayed. The friendly landscape turned traitor. The rock gave way. The tree renounced its hold. I hurtled downward. Seconds later, here I am, lying smashed on the bottom of the same ravine that had beckoned me to safety.

I'm alive. I had not expected it to be so.

Reeling with the shock of the impact, I struggle to sit up. I begin to assess the damage. There is blood on the rock around me. My blood. I feel my face. A front tooth has snapped off. My nose is smashed. One wrist resists bending, and several fingers stick out at odd angles. None of them appear to be broken. I look piece by piece at the rest of my body, patting it gently with my hands as though to assure myself that I am all still here. There is a ten-inch long oozing scrape on my right thigh. Multiple bruises and cuts cover the rest of my body. My left hip brings excruciating pain when I attempt to shift it. My own bone protrudes through the skin below my right knee, with muscle and sinew exposed to the air and flesh shredded around it. Both legs are useless: limp as last night's ramen. I cannot move either one so much as an inch.

I appraise my situation. I am seriously injured. I cannot walk, crawl, or even stand up. I am in the most remote area of Kings Canyon National Park, deep in the back country of the Sierra Nevada. I am at least twenty-five grueling miles from the nearest trailhead. I had selected the Tehipite Valley for just this reason, having craved the magnificent solitude of the furthermost reaches of the wilderness for my solo journey. I have not seen a soul for two days.

Only a handful of people hike in this valley each season, the rangers told me. I had lost the overgrown path shortly before I fell, so I am off trail. Even if hikers do pass by, they will not see me. My friends and family do not expect me back for five or six more days, so they will not yet post a search. I do not carry a cell phone, and in any case, no signal can reach into the depths of this ravine. I am utterly alone in an untraveled portion of the back country. My chances for survival are grim. But I am still alive.

2

For Love of the Mountains

I am often suffused with longing to be in the mountains, as I make my way through ordinary life: working, paying taxes, running errands, completing jobs. Something akin to homesickness sweeps over me, bringing tears to forgotten places behind my eyes, causing my skin to tingle with desire for the feel of mountain air and my soul to cry out at the deprivation.

Now, stranded and helpless, I am still feeling my love for this place. Whispering leaves conspire to distract me. Birds call out songs of beauty for my ears. The sounds, the smells, the very feel of the air comfort me. I recall the glorious places that I have been in just these two previous weeks. I am desolate to think that I may not live to climb the mountains again; even if I am saved, I may lose my legs. But the beauty here reminds me also of the glorious splendors of life, and for that, I want to live.

My mind wanders to the past, to the year when my love affair with the Sierra began. An awkward sixteen years of age, I was coming newly into my womanhood, uncertain in the world and uneasy in my self. I was about to embark upon my very first backpacking trip. My Dad had organized this excursion with his customary enthusiasm. He and I, and my thirteen-year-old brother Daniel, had driven 3,000 miles across the United States to be here. We had navigated twenty-five nar- row miles of ancient logging road—698 curves in all—before arriving at our destination, a sub-alpine valley in Sequoia National Park. This singular valley was a family legend. We seemed worlds away from the

Baltimore suburb where I was born and raised. I had grown up knowing about the beauty of this place, seeing the glint in my father's eyes whenever he spoke of it, and longing to see it for myself.

Mineral King. Even crushed in my ravine, distracted by the constant pain in my body and desperately worried about the future, a vision of the place in my mind's eye is enough to send tremors of longing through my being. I can see it as if I am there, a magnificent glacial canyon carved from centuries of shifting and reforming ice, a monument to the persistent powers of nature. I envision it green from springtime rains and snowmelt, an abundance of wildflowers spilling over the trails in riotous glory. Up from the valley floor surge the looming peaks of the Great Western Divide, cradling the valley on three sides. Farewell Gap beckons from the south; Franklin Pass rises to the southeast. I can smell wild sage and granite dust; hear the merry gurgle of clear, snow-fed brooks.

It was there, in Mineral King, that I came to know the mountains, to know myself, to appreciate the powers of my body, and to encounter within my own character the determination that would serve me in years to come. It was there that I fell in love with the Sierra.

Mineral King from Farewell Gap.

It was 1972. The summer morning was bright with sunshine. Standing with my family in the dirt parking lot near the trailhead, I was worried. I was often anxious in those days, concerned about nothing more specific than the unknown. On that particular day, I knew what it was that troubled me. Unsure if I could face the rigors of the journey ahead, I dreaded the coming trip.

At sixteen, I was scrawny and shy, partially developed, and embarrassed about the changes in my body. My dad had dressed us all in men's clothing, with an eye toward thrift and durability. Our gear was sturdy and functional but did nothing to enhance the tentative self-image of a young woman. I was quick to assign any lack of fit to the inadequacies of my own body, and I hid myself beneath the ill-tailored male garb. My long hair was skinned back in a pigtail, and with my flat chest, cowering slouch, and masculine clothes, I was often mistaken for a boy.

From my customary position as bystander, I watched clusters of backpackers at their cars. I saw the easy way they swung their packs onto their backs, the cheerful camaraderie, the bounce in their stride and the strong, well-formed legs that would carry them and their gear away up fertile trails toward places of hidden beauty. I noted the laughter and bright smiles of the women, exuding confidence as they hiked off on long tanned limbs. I admired their tall, fit-looking companions. All of them had the strength and assurance that I lacked. I watched with envy and reverence. They were everything that I was not.

My unformed images of who I wanted to be began to crystallize during those moments in the clear air. I wanted to live my life in places like that. I wanted to be with those backpackers, swinging along with nimble strength, capable and happy and unafraid. I wanted to be like them. I wanted to be one of them.

We had been planning this trip for months. My dad had outfitted us carefully. We wore jeans and long sleeved plaid cotton shirts over T-shirts. Wide brimmed Amish straw hats protected our faces from the sun. We had rugged leather boots laced onto our feet, with traditional Ragg Wool socks, and liners to prevent blisters. All three of us carried army surplus rucksacks on our backs. They were olive green canvas, with two shoulder straps angling out in a V shape from the top middle of the pack, no frames or inserts or hip belts or pockets or gear loops.

We each had a sleeping bag and a thin foam mattress strapped to the top of our packs. We carried a Sierra cup hooked onto our belts, handy for drinking from the many streams. Sturdy crewneck Navy watch sweaters made of serviceable dark blue wool were our only warm clothing, and a bandana served a multitude of purposes. My dad had a little Optimus stove and a billy-tin, a small pot with a clip-on lid. He carried a snakebite kit. We took dried food for ten days. My father had found us detachable, fluorescent orange shoulder pads for comfort, and made sure that we each had a ChapStick lip moisturizer in our pocket, so that our lips wouldn't become raw in the dry mountain air.

We didn't take much else. We had very little gear by twenty-first century standards. We had no water sandals, no tents or bivies, no fleece or microfiber clothing. The bears were not savvy in the ways of humans, so hanging food from a tree would be adequate deterrence: no need to carry a bear canister. The brooks still ran with pure, uncontaminated water, so there was no thought of filtering it. We didn't trouble ourselves with nonessentials such as flashlights, changes of clothing, towels or rain gear. We had what we needed. My dad had hiked these mountains for years with less than we now carried. We felt ourselves to be quite adequately equipped, and so we were.

The one luxury that I did take with me was a paperback novel. Rosemary Rogers' *Sweet Savage Love* was a historical romance about a young woman who suffered perpetual hardship as she traveled through the pages of westward expansion and the Mexican Revolution. Though gently bred, she was forever sleeping under wagons and in woods, always feminine, always radiantly beautiful and forever spirited and sensual no matter what fate life had dealt her. I carried that paperback with me as a talisman and hid my face in it whenever the rigors of the trail became too much for me. My brother hated the book and gleefully burned the pages when I was done with them. But I admired the plucky heroine. The romantic vision of beauty and true love in the wilderness did much to get me through the hardships of the trip.

The straps of my pack dug painfully into my inexperienced shoulders. My leg muscles strained with protest, unaccustomed to the severe climbs presented by the Sierra. I panted in the thin air. Our sleeping bags were sufficient against the icy, high-country nights, but my feet were always cold. I shivered with chill in the frosty morning air and sweated buckets under the hot midday sun. I was exhausted and hungry and smelly and cranky. I hated the trip. I hated myself. I didn't think I could make it. But I went on.

Giving up did not seem to be an option. My family had long favored a tradition of excellence at conquering the odds. *Snatching victory from the jaws of defeat*, my parents called it. We took pride in being smarter and more determined than the rest, in achieving victory despite peril and privation.

I had learned to value hardship. In order to attain maximal enjoyment from any conquest, defeat had to be an imminent possibility. The tougher the hardship that had to be overcome, the sweeter would be the triumph. Sometimes this inspired me to seek out particularly difficult situations, believing that greater satisfaction was intrinsic to a higher degree of challenge. I had learned to regard hardship as a necessary enhancement to the euphoria of success.

Amy at sixteen, backpacking with her brother, Dan, and father, William C. Neelands. August 1972.

I had also learned to value success. The tenacity and determination inspired by my parents' adage served me well in demanding circumstances. I understood that sometimes one had to work hard to achieve one's goal. No matter how bad things looked, victory might still be near at hand. I would not give up.

I had never excelled in physical education class. At my public high school, it had been decided that the appropriate gym outfits for young ladies were little yellow dresses with cap sleeves, short flared skirts, and yellow bloomers. Nobody looked good in this getup, and I looked sillier than most, having already reached an unladylike height, with a round middle and gangly arms and legs. Thus attired, we were sent to run about the field with lacrosse sticks or baseball mitts. My face would flush an unattractive shade of red at any sign of physical exertion, and my eyes would not coordinate with my hands. I was usually one of the last to be chosen for any team.

The one physical thing I could do was walk. We were a one-car family, and my dad took the car to work. My mom and we three kids walked wherever we needed to go. My earliest memories include walking to the grocery store, gazing up at my mom, tall above me, and holding onto her hand. Sometimes we took the bus, but we would play a game to see if we could get to the next bus stop before the bus came. We would race the bus for blocks, occasionally covering the entire route just for the fun of it.

As we grew older, we walked for miles, at times setting out with a destination in mind, other times seeking the sheer joy of discovery. Our suburb opened easily into farmland in those days, and a half mile or so took you to lengths of country road, vacant fields, and uncivilized streams full of fascinating slimy creatures; wondrous places only reached by foot. We walked to do errands, to go shopping. We walked to our schools, we walked to visit friends, and to the local swimming holes. It gave me pleasure to cover the miles with my lanky legs, but I didn't give it much thought. We had always walked.

Now, on my first backpacking trip, I continued to walk. I knew from years of covering ground that if I put one foot in front of the other, I would eventually get to where I wanted to go. And so I did. Up over 11,680-foot Franklin Pass we plodded, and down into Upper Rattlesnake Canyon. We covered eleven and a half miles that first punishing day, tackling a 3,850-foot climb. On we went the next day, past the Upper and Lower Rattlesnakes, and eventually to the Kern River. There we turned south, arriving finally at the rustic Kern Canyon Ranger Station, in the Kern River Canyon. We enjoyed the respite of a layover, dayhiking and fishing in Golden Trout Creek. A few days later, we headed back out over Coyote Pass and Farewell Gap. Our loop was about forty-six miles.

Despite the hardships, or perhaps because of them, I began to appreciate the life that consumed us. The cold hard ground felt welcome after a rough day's hiking. Each ray of sunshine on a chilly morning was to be celebrated. I was hungry enough so that the dried food tasted delicious. I liked rinsing out my clothing in icy water and hunting for sticks of firewood. Best of all, I grew stronger by the day. I felt the blood coursing through my body. I enjoyed using the new muscles in my arms and legs. I didn't worry much about how I looked. Instead I watched what was around me. I began to see the panoramic landscapes, the statuesque groves of sequoia and pine, the clear sparkling air that coaxed blades of grass and wildflowers into a luminescence brighter than I had ever imagined. The place spoke to my soul. And when, after ten magnificent days, we arrived triumphantly back at the trailhead, I could understand why my dad loved this most special of places. The trip had been the most wonderful experience of my life.

3

On the Trail of the Ancestors

Perhaps I love these places because they are part of my heritage. I have a few faded photos: black and white likenesses of hardy, determined-looking ancestors hiking in some of my own favorite places. I walk upon the same trails that were there a hundred years ago. I place my feet upon the very same spots that my grandmother's feet have touched.

*Lucia Starkey Neelands (Amy's grandmother) hiking
in the Sierra between 1906 and 1910.*

The mountains seem timeless to me, a backdrop for the flowing of generations, unhurried yet constant in their changing formation. I imagine that long after I am vanished from this planet, the Sierra will still stand, majestic and powerful. I fancy becoming a part of that enduring legacy, living some of my own life amidst this gift to posterity.

Grateful for the strength of my robust ancestors, I have the same sturdy Irish legs, the same indomitable determination, the same affinity for the mountains. The resilient forebears who roamed this part of

Amy's dad, William C. Neelands, hiking in the Sierra as a boy.

the earth before I came are long gone, but their story is a part of my own.

William L. Neelands and Lucia Starkey Neelands, my Father's parents, had frequented the Sierra back country since 1909, spending long summers wandering the mountains, exploring the same trails that I love to walk. They were known as ardent naturalists and guardians of the mountain tradition. Like me, my family had delighted in seeking the less traveled paths. Surely they would have been drawn to a place like the Tehipite.

This August afternoon in 2003, stranded in the ravine in a space between life and death, I feel the spirits of my ancestors drawing close. Perhaps they have been to this very spot. I wonder if they have wandered here, but I do not have any evidence.

A year later, in an old photo album, I find it: A scrawled mountain log in my Grandmother's hand that says simply *1924 — Tehipite.* The Tehipite had lured them too. They had been there.

My Dad, William C. Neelands, was born in 1913. At four, he was old enough to ride on a burro, and my grandparents simply brought him along. Faded snap shots of the Sierra show a little Bill, playing happily amongst granite boulders with the Great Western Divide behind him.

In 1935, the Neelands family took over the management of Lewis Camp, now the site of the Kern Canyon Ranger Station. It was operated at that time as a privately owned camp for wayfarers within the boundaries of Sequoia National Park, adjacent to Kings Canyon Park. Jules Conterno had retained a lifetime tenancy when the Park system annexed the area in 1926, and now he turned the camp's management over to my relatives. Lewis Camp had been a back country encampment for over sixty years. No road had ever scarred the way into the Kern, and the area was still blessed with limited access. Lewis Camp was a worthy rest stop, attracting quite a crowd of hikers, rangers and mountain people. The back country way-station was renowned for well-told tales around friendly campfires, mouth-watering meals, and the engaging personalities of the Neelands family.

Always my father's face would glow when he talked of summers in the Sierra. He loved the mountains, speaking with passion about days in the Kern River Canyon and his weekend habit of hiking back to Silver City. It was a good twenty-five miles one way. He'd do it in a day, arriving in Silver City in time for the Saturday Night Dances, and hiking back the following morning to work all week. I would guess, from the way that he spoke of those days, that they were the very best times of his life.

In 1946, my dad returned to California, fresh from an Army stint in the Philippines. His own father died shortly afterward, and he and his aging mother took over the running of Lewis Camp, leasing it again from Jules Conterno. Job demands moved my father to the East Coast just two years later. He stayed on the East Coast, met my mom, also from California, and raised a family. But he never forgot the years in the back country. He never forgot the Sierra.

My father has been gone now for almost twenty years. I imagine that I hear his words, affectionate and sometimes chastising.

"Oh, Amy," he would say with fond amusement, if he knew of my current pickle. Then he would start thinking of a way out. The twinkle of light on the streamlet next to me reminds me of the sparkle in his eyes when he talked about the high country. Now he too has become a part of these places. In 1986 my brother and I hiked in to Sequoia to fulfill his final wishes. We scattered his ashes at the site of Lewis Camp in the Kern River Canyon.

I know my father would have expected me to live as he and my kinfolk had done, undaunted by misfortune, reliant upon their own gritty determination. Stranded now in the ravine, in my time of need, I draw upon the strength of my predecessors. They were undeniably unconventional. And they were adventurous. Certainly there were challenges. Simply getting to the mountains was an accomplishment in the early twentieth century, and for back country travel, my relatives had none of the high-tech gear that today's hiker finds essential. I feel in myself the temperament of people for whom hardship is a worthy price to pay for the inestimable joy of days in the wilderness. Surely these rugged people would not have given up without a fight.

I fancy that I hear the murmurs of angelic voices echoing across the rocks of the ravine. Perhaps my long-gone ancestors are looking for me. Will I live to follow those trails again, or will my ghost join theirs and whisper in peaceful contentment through trees and canyons? I like the etheric voices. I hear them murmuring around me like the flutter of gentle wings. I am comforted.

4

The Trip of a Lifetime

It was my custom to spend some time alone in the wilderness each year, to clear my mind and renew my relationship with myself. I would grow weary of urban living and the perils of human interaction, and head out into the back country for restoration.

Each summer, I wrestled a piece of time out of my busy schedule to spend in the wilderness, blocking it out on my calendar and defending it aggressively against the encroaching demands of work, summertime recreation, friends, parenthood. Each year as I hiked, I devoured the information on my maps, planning and replanning, counting out miles, lusting after faraway spots, wondering how far I could go and what might be just over the next pass, around the next mountain. I always wanted more.

In the summer of 2003, I was particularly happy with the plan for my trip. With my work life stabilized and my sixteen-year-old son almost grown, I had managed to carve out a nice block of time. At forty-six years old, I was stronger than I had ever been. Two and a half weeks previously, I had completed a 120-mile loop in Northern California's Henry W. Coe State Park as a training hike. Now I was eager for my annual trek to Sequoia/Kings Canyon, my family mecca. I had often hiked in these national parks, but this year I especially looked forward to exploring territory unfamiliar to me.

I had planned an ambitious loop, a challenging hike that would take me to the Pacific Crest Trail, through glacial canyons, deep valleys and sub-alpine meadows, past groves of giant Sequoia, around crystal clear lakes, into sprawling expanses waist-high with wildflowers, across rushing streamlets and over tumbles of huge granite boulders. I planned to hike a portion of the John Muir Trail, climbing Pinchot Pass, breathtaking Mather Pass, famous Muir Pass, and frolicking through the many meadows of Evolution Valley. Best of all, my trip would take me to the almost inaccessible Middle Fork Kings River, nestled in the remote Tehipite Valley.

The great twin canyons of the south and middle forks of the Kings River, ranging from 4,000 to almost 8,000 feet in depth, dominate Kings Canyon National Park and furrow the already rugged Sierra with their fantastic forms. To travel through these rock-lined recesses is to explore some of the roughest terrain in North America.

Several years ago, I read these words in William Tweed's *Sequoia Kings Canyon: The Story Behind the Scenery.* The book is a lovely volume

Amy getting ready to leave on her big hike. July 2003. Photo by Adrian Morgan.

filled with unforgettable Sierra photographs, but the words were what captured my imagination and inspired my determined fantasies. I knew from the moment that I read these phrases that I wanted to go to the Tehipite. 2003 was the year that I would realize that dream.

I loaded my pack and set off on my long-awaited journey, leaving home behind me. I drove the several hours to Fresno, a fairly grim place in my estimation, and then turned east, up into the foothills. A couple more hours of travel found me camped in the national forest at about 8,000 feet, getting acclimated to the higher elevation. Up late in my tent, I pored over topographical maps with my flashlight and did a final check of the contents of my pack. I was excited, anticipating the wondrous sights. So many beautiful places! The next morning, I drove past Cedar Grove to Roads End trailhead and parked my car, checking it carefully for anything that might attract bears or thieves. I planned to get my wilderness permit that morning, never having needed a reservation for just one person.

The young ranger in the office at the trailhead sat at a desk, routinely handing out permits, giving advice and warning novice backpackers about the dangers and etiquette of life on the trail. He scanned my itinerary, a printout on a crumpled piece of paper. It was long, and scrawled with careful revisions. I had planned a loop that covered sixty-six miles of trail, taking me over seven passes and through some of the most magnificent and remote scenery in Kings Canyon National Park. The ranger looked again.

"Wow. This is the trip of a lifetime." Somehow the clichéd words took on new meaning as he gazed up at me with the glint of the enlightened in his eyes. He had been been to these places. He had seen the wonders that I sought. We talked animatedly for a while, with him pointing out favored spots, me asking a few questions about trail and creek crossings, excited by the start of my trip. Another group came in, and his attention was drawn away. I took my permit, smiled my goodbye and went on my way. Neither one of us knew how incredible the journey would really be.

Mine was an ambitious route, and I wanted to allow myself plenty of time for contingencies. I didn't include layover days. My preference was to keep moving, to enjoy the ever-changing panorama of scenery, to stop where I was inspired and hike on if I wished. Security was in knowing that wherever I went, everything necessary was in the pack on my back. An easy hike was six or seven miles, and those days I considered to be rest days. I could do eighteen miles a day over rugged terrain if I had to, and though I didn't plan any days to be that long, I included some twelve-and fourteen-mile treks. My restless soul was satisfied by the promise of new vistas with each dawn. There was much to see, and I wanted to experience it all.

In my planning phase, I had approximated the distances as best I could, aided by a good topographical map with mileage figures. I had factored in a couple of extra days, as I always did, in case I had under-estimated my endurance or the demands of unknown trails. There were many uncertainties in the wilderness, and I didn't want anyone to worry if I was not back exactly when I intended. When I returned, I would call my friends and family from the trail head to let them know I was safe.

This was my planned itinerary:
Day 1: Cedar Grove/Roads End trailhead past Mist Falls (4.5)
Day 2: Paradise Valley (8)
Day 3: Paradise Valley to John Muir/Pacific Crest Trail (8.8)
Day 4: North past Pinchot Mountain, over Pinchot Pass (10.2)
Day 5: Upper basin, over Mather Pass (16.2)
Day 6: Past Le Conte Canyon, Past Muir Pass (12.3)
Day 7: Junction with Goddard Canyon Trail (11.0)
Day 8: Muir Trail Ranch (7.1) Toward Florence Lake (3.0)
Day 9: Thompson Pass (9.3)
Day 10: Big Maxson Meadow (12.7)
Day 11: Crown Pass to Crown Valley (12.9)
Day 12: Tehipite Valley (11.7)
Day 13: Tehipite Valley to Simpson Meadow (10)
Day 14: Extra Day
Day 15: Lake of the Fallen Moon (10.0)
Day 16: To Roads End (14.8)
Day 17: Camp in National Forest

I intended to start at Roads End, just past Cedar Grove. That trail-head would launch me immediately into Kings Canyon National Park. I planned to climb gently through Paradise Valley on the Bubbs Creek Trail for the first two days, attracted by the promise of the name. I then would turn north at Woods Creek, joining the John Muir Trail for the next fifty-six miles and climbing Pinchot, Mather, and Muir Passes sequentially. I had seen pictures of the spectacular metamorphic peaks and incomparable lakes stair-stepping up toward Muir Pass, and I'd long wanted to see Evolution Valley, a long, park-like sprawl on the

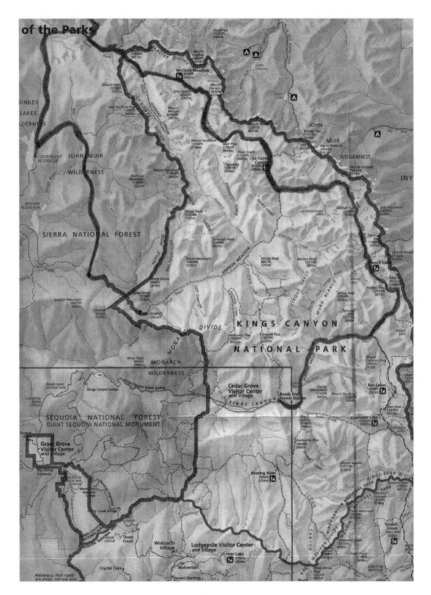

Map of Amy's route.

other side. Shortly before the Muir Trail Ranch, I would leave the Muir Trail and head east, then south, to make my trip a loop, working my way over several more minor passes through the Dinkey Lakes and John Muir Wilderness Areas, and bits of Sequoia National Park. Circling back west into Kings Canyon National Park, I would descend into the Tehipite via a much switchbacked track that leads finally to the legendary Middle Fork. I would wander for a couple of days through the valley, then attack the brutal climb out from Simpson Meadow over Granite Pass, and finally make the dramatic descent that would take me back to Roads End. It was an inspired plan. Studying the rugged peaks and many miles of trail on my topo map, I fairly drooled in anticipation.

5

Before the Fall

As I hiked along, buoyant with joy over the start of my trip, I would stop often to enjoy new panoramas and to view small delights; a cluster of tiny flowers, a uniquely formed leaf, a lizard doing push-ups on a sunny rock. Sometimes I'd pause to sit and reflect, thoughts freed from the expected mind patterns of civilized life. Or I'd stop to write, words flowing out unrestricted like the gushing melody of mountain streams. I kept a trail log of these mental meanderings.

Day 1: I leave the ranger station at Roads End and head up Paradise Valley, joining groups of backpackers and throngs of day hikers headed for Mist Falls. A young woman asks if she can have some sunscreen. Reluctantly, I tell her no, explaining that I have just two ounces that I have allotted myself for the next eighteen days. I'll need it more than she will.

I pass a group of four people heading back toward the trailhead at Roads End.

"Where've you been?" I ask cheerfully, always eager to exchange information with other backpackers.

"Oh, we were going to do the whole loop," said one woman. They had planned to do the forty-six mile Rae Lakes loop, and had been chased back early by mosquitoes.

"The worst mosquitoes I've ever seen," the woman explains.

"They'll bite through anything. We have to go back." She is eager for me to understand the severity of the hardship that has driven them in. They don't ask where I am headed, and I don't tell them.

Camping that night at Upper Paradise—a paradise only if you are a mosquito—I see a sodden sleeping bag abandoned on a log in mute testimony to more discomforts of the backwoods life. I sleep soundly, undaunted by insects and moisture. The next day I continue on.

Day 3: Pleased to be a day ahead of schedule, I turn north onto the John Muir Trail (JMT). I now leave the easier loop trails, which often attract tenderfoot backpackers out for a few days or a long weekend. I begin to encounter through-hikers on the popular JMT Yosemite to Whitney hike, 222 rugged miles of some of the most beautiful terrain in the world. This is a demanding route, and attracts a certain sort of tough, determined backpacker. By the time they get to where I am, they have already been on the go for a couple of weeks, trail-worn and exultant, full of tales of their trips.

We talk about life on the trail and swap adventure stories. The usual standards of conversational etiquette seem not to apply. Rarely does anyone ask, "What do you do?" It simply is not relevant. The wilderness is the great equalizer. The experience we share is the bond between us. Often we do not even get around to learning one another's names. A common question is "Have you seen any bears?" We discuss bear sightings. We talk about the trail ahead and where we've come from. We compare pack weights and chat about our gear. We brag about the lightness of our packs. We share visions of hot showers and re-entry meals. We love to talk about what we have to eat, and what sorts of tasty foods we will get when we return to civilization. Long-distance hikers are typically on tight rations, as am I. We fantasize voraciously about the culinary comforts we've left behind. We compare trail conditions. I always ask about the Tehipite, but few of the through hikers have heard of it.

Day 4: The small satisfactions of life on the trail bring moments of joy. Squatting by a granite boulder, feeling the wind tickle my bare butt as the scent of hot pee rises, steaming from the pine needles. Finding that I can produce a reasonable facsimile of cappuccino by shaking instant coffee and powdered milk vigorously in my water bottle. Shade when it's hot. Rays of sunshine to cut the morning chill.

I recall my dream to hike the Pacific Crest Trail. It's a heady goal, requiring an entire summer of rigorous hiking. The last time I thought of it, I was sidetracked by marriage and motherhood. Now my son is nearly grown, and that goal again seems possible. I begin mentally weighing my supplies, my food, my stamina…I bet I can do it.

Day 5: I'm pushing myself hard. Each day involves a climb of 3,000 to 4,000 feet. I've fallen a day behind. How was it that I thought I could do three passes in three days? Never mind. I have allowed an extra day with just such a possibility in mind. I am tired, but each day's hiking is more magnificent than the day before.

I cook my favorite back country meal, sushi. I have sheets of dry nori seaweed, already cut into little pieces, about four inches square. I roll them into cones, prop them in my pot, and fill them with minute rice. I garnish with dried onions or chives and reconstituted dried tuna. A little soy sauce completes the feast. Yummy!

Day 6: It has rained every single day since I left. Heavy, frequent rains are most unusual in the Sierra in the summertime. In all my years of hiking here, I have rarely experienced more than an isolated afternoon shower. Often I hike for weeks without any sign of a downpour. Now, clouds gather daily to release torrents of water at a moment's notice. Nights are usually wet as well. I don't have full rain gear, but it doesn't matter. I deal with the rain, setting up my tarp as a shelter during the worst of it, making cups of hot tea and reading my book until the showers pass. Or I hike on, using my tarp as a poncho and pack cover. Some days the sun never comes out. Everybody I meet is wet and dirty. Nobody has been able to do laundry for days. Hikers sport soggy, half-dried clothing hanging from their packs as they tromp along. I haven't washed my hair in a week. We all smell pretty funky. Someone tries to apologize. We talk him down. We're all in this together.

Today, I reach Muir Pass. Lingering for a couple of hours at the hut on top, I make tea and dry out a bit during a spot of sunshine. The rocks around the hut are draped with other backpackers' socks and shirts. Clouds are gathering, but I can't decide which way they are moving. Finally I pack up and head down into the next basin. Twenty minutes or so after I hike on, the clouds open, and gallons of water pour down upon me. Worse yet, lightning flashes and thunder cracks at the same moment, striking the peaks around the basin that surrounds me.

It is too far to go back to the hut. Way up above timberline, with not a tree in sight, I am clearly the most moist and metallic thing around,

Amy at Muir Hut. July 29, 2003, six days before the fall. Photo by Cari.

and taller than any of the nearby rocks. I toss my metal pole aside. Thankfully there is no metal frame in my pack. I pull it close to me and throw myself flat on the ground, yanking my waterproof tarp over me. Peeking out, I can see lightning strike the closest peaks. It begins to hail great pea-sized rounds of ice. They pile up around and over me. I tremble in abject terror each time the thunder cracks over me. I fully expect to be struck by lightning at any second.

Forty-five minutes later, the storm moves past and the sun comes out, melting the heaps of hailstones. I hike on, drying out as I walk along.

Another hiker tells me that "they" are using airplanes to seed the gathering clouds, creating extreme conditions here but ensuring an adequate water supply for the Los Angeles area. Great.

Day 7: My hipbones have re-emerged from a layer of winter-lazy fat. The hip belt of my pack hugs them gently like the casual caress of an old friend. My body sways softly to its own rhythm as I walk along.

Occasionally I'm overcome by the urge to write, stopping on a chunk of granite to scrawl furiously: my impressions, a sudden epiphany, a few anecdotes from life on the trail.

I am hungry. I have packed food carefully, but not planned to re-supply along the way. I eat adequately, but not abundantly. I tend to forget the extreme caloric requirements of a trip such as mine. I calculate I'd need around 4,000 to 5,000 calories a day, but I'm not willing to carry that much food weight. I tighten my belt a bit and dream of high calorie goodies.

I climb past three slightly plump ladies who seem a bit overburdened. They are hiking out early, having been part of a support team for a man who is running the entire Muir Trail. The rain has discouraged them. I talk with them for a while, and they insist on donating some unnecessary food from their heavy packs, delighted not to have to carry it all out. I in turn am pleased by the extra supplies, and accept Clif Bar energy food bars, freeze-dried turkey tetrazzini, peas, peanut M&Ms candy, squashed marshmallows, ramen, and powdered chicken soup.

I am short on a few luxury items. My flashlight battery has proven to be defective. I could use a bit more bug repellent and some extra matches. I begin to ask folks along the way about the places I have yet to pass. I hear that Florence Lake boasts a snack bar on the far side. I know that the Muir Trail Ranch has a small store. I ask one family what the store has to offer.

"Not much," says the mom.

"It's very small," says the dad.

"It's wonderful!" says the daughter. "They'll have everything you need!" Of the three reports, I decide to believe hers.

Day 8: I arrive at the Muir Trail Ranch. A charming little store, appearing to have been there for a hundred years or more, staffed by a woman at least as old, does indeed offer up everything I might need, except for additional food supplies. They stock just one or two of each essential, some things dusty with age, everything reasonably priced. The wizened little woman who runs the place gives me a free flashlight and supplies me with batteries, bug repellent, a lighter, and a brochure about "Backpacking in the Sierra Nevada" evidently printed in the 1950s. It lists pack weights for a family of three. The man is to carry forty-four pounds. The eleven-year-old boy takes fourteen pounds. The woman has just ten and a half. The cover price says thirty-five cents.

"How much is it?" I ask.

"Whatever it says." She replies. I hand over my change, thinking that the pamphlet has probably been there for fifty years. I consider buying a T-shirt just so I will have something clean and dry, but decide not. I head across the river for a delightful sojourn in the hot springs at Blayney Meadows.

Still dreaming of candy bars, I decide to detour slightly off-route toward Florence Lake. I can't get much information, but it seems that there is a ferry to the other side.

Day 9: I catch the ferry, a little motorboat about ten feet long. At the snack bar, I wolf down Twinkies snack cakes, a burrito, and a can of V8 vegetable juice. I stock up on cheese and chocolate bars, and purchase a little clock meant to hang from a zipper pull. I ride the ferry back across.

I've turned off the JMT now, traveling lesser known trails. Good. The scenery along the popular route was lovely, but I was passing around fifty hikers a day—too many people to be a genuine back country experience—and the trail and campsites show the wear from the many passersby. Not my idea of wilderness. I'm enjoying the solitude of this less popular area.

Day 10: I am lost. I camped last night at a lake unknown to me, having somehow missed the route toward Thompson Pass. It's a lovely little lake, perfect in every detail. A pool of clear water nestles by a sparkling granite cliff. On the opposite shore, a grove of giant sequoias leads to a gentle sandy beach, tucked in beside a little meadow waving soft green grasses. I continue on, using my compass to direct me south on an unidentified trail. My map tells me that I should run into a jeep road today.

Found it! Now I know where I am. The jeep road, the only one of its kind anywhere around, plunges steeply down and will lead me south to Courtright Reservoir. From there I can get myself back on track and continue with my loop.

About midday, several four-wheel drive vehicles rumble past. The tires are huge, maybe four feet in height. The trucks, piled high with gas cans and coolers and camping equipment, strain up the steep incline, engines growling as they rumble over boulders and ruts as big as my body. The drivers look at me like they've seen a ghost, then tip their hats politely. How must I appear to them, a lone woman, materializing suddenly out of the wilderness?

I find the reservoir. It seems an ugly place to me, skeletal bits of dead tree-trunk sticking out of the water at grim angles. After skirting Courtright Reservoir for a while, in a rustic campground I meet a family who has just come up from the Tehipite. There are three of them, a man, a woman, and a teenage girl. I question them eagerly. I want to know if the trail is difficult to follow. They assure me that although overgrown, it is quite passable. They talk with delight about the Valley. I ask about the Kings River crossing, concerned that constant rain will have made the passage dangerous. They happily share their information, telling me where the river broadens into shallows and I can cross safely. They walk me to my next trail junction, and wave goodbye.

I pass a solo hiker who has made his own lightweight pack. After we chat for a while, he tells me where he has seen two almost-new garbage bags, probably blown away from a large encampment by a river. He has folded them carefully and placed them under a rock. I already have two garbage bags, but I find the windfall and take the bags along with me just in case.

Day 11: "But what do you do all day?" friends often ask me. They are genuinely curious, unable to imagine days and weeks spent without the demands of a job, the solace of events and entertainments, and most of all, without other people.

Mostly I hike. As I walk along, comforted by the steady motion, I admire the continually changing scenes before me. Sweeping vistas across glacial canyons give way to rippling streamlets surrounded by cool clusters of wildflowers, opening into peaceful forests. There is much to appreciate and enjoy. I take frequent small breaks, to apply sunscreen or bug repellent, to take off or put on an article of clothing, to enjoy some especially beautiful spot, take care of a personal need, or engage in some primal awareness. I stop to hear the silence and to feel my own blood racing through my body. Every moment carries its own delights. The moments build into hours, and the days flow by. I am never bored and rarely lonely.

Day 12: My trail log says simply CRASH!

The Day of the Fall

Day 12, August the fourth, is a glorious day. I awaken where I camped last night at dusk, next to a large meadow frequented by new fawns, partway between Crown Pass and Crown Valley. A lovely place!

My rain tarp, stretched taut between three scrubby trees and my hiking pole, has served me well, shielding me from the rain despite the night's showers. My site is rocky enough to drain adequately, and provides easy access to the trail of the morning, climbing gently up the hillside behind me. Very shortly the sun peeks over a ridge top.

The day starts out as a day in the back country often does. Clambering out of my down bag, clad only in black silk long johns, I shiver in the chill air. I scramble hastily into my pants and shirt and jacket, (appreciating the extra warmth that the dampish clothing offers) tug on my boots, loosely laced, and go off to pee behind a handy bush. Nobody around to see me.

I light up my little stove. I had purified enough water the night before, stashing it conveniently in bottles near my camp, so within a few minutes I am warming my hands and tummy with the luxurious heat of a scalding cup of coffee. Instant has never tasted so good. I add a little powdered coconut milk that I'd saved for some special morning. A cup of oatmeal with raisins and cashews completes my breakfast. I spread things around on agreeable chunks of granite and wait for everything to dry. Life is perfect.

Carefully, I sort my food supplies. I do this every day, counting and figuring, enjoying planning what to have for the next meal, and making certain that I have ample supplies for the rest of my journey. It's all part of the fun.

The Tehipite Valley. Photo by Jake Van Akkeren, August 2003.

Hopping up occasionally to turn over drying gear, I next study my map and trail log to check the mileage to today's destination. Factoring in a couple of extra detours, I figure I've completed about 129 spectacular miles. I have about forty to go. I'm right on schedule with four or five more days left. I'm averaging a little over eleven and a half miles a day, and I fret a bit about that. My own harshest critic, I tell myself I should be doing more.

Today's trip starts me out with an undemanding three miles to Crown Valley. Then I head down. The first six miles of this next segment look easy. The second chunk, switching back and forth from the rim right down into the Tehipite, takes me from 7,500 to 4,100 feet of elevation in just three miles. There isn't room on my map for either the topo lines or the many switchbacks, so tightly are they packed in, but I can figure the statistics. This is a very steep trail by anyone's estimation. My twelve-mile day will bring me gently to rest at the bottom of the valley in the very core of Kings Canyon National Park. I can hardly wait.

I pack up my gear, and as the day is warming rapidly, I change into shorts and tank top for hiking. I keep my long-sleeved shirt over the tank top, lace my boots securely, give my map a last glance, and swing my pack onto my back. I've tucked today's lunch and snacks into a handy pocket on my pack, and I carry a liter of filtered water with me. Whistling happily to myself, I cover the trail in long leggy strides, eating up the miles with the joy of my own strength.

Proud of my independence and enchanted by my adventure, I whistle as I walk, cheerful snatches of tune. Releasing small gusts of music as I breathe in and out, the notes gurgle forth semiconsciously with my breath like the melody of a soul in tune with itself.

I've lost a few pounds, and certainly gained some muscle. I wear black shorts today, and my favorite olive green tanktop, thinking to increase my sun exposure so that when I get back, my friends will ooh and ah at how tanned and fit I am, after my expedition.

I already feel the triumph of achievement. Given my early imprinting, this sort of trip suits me well. There has indeed been some hardship. I have struggled over high mountain passes; lungs gasping for air, muscles straining, skin suffering the inevitable cuts, bruises, and mosquito bites; pushing myself to my edges, undaunted by inclement weather and unexpected difficulties. Marveling at the places I have been and at the wondrous sights that I have seen, I am well-pleased with my journey. I feel justifiably proud of myself. Victory will be mine.

I am headed for the highlight of my trip, the Tehipite Valley. For years now I have wanted to experience this secluded place, to commune alone with the beauty and wildness that few people ever witness. A couple of days amidst the glories of this remote valley, then I tackle the 8,000-foot climb and the rugged descent that will eventually take me back to my car at the trailhead and the luxuries that I have begun to miss.

My energy is good. I always hike best in the morning. Surging along the short track that takes me to Crown Valley, I notice a small camp with a couple of rustic cabins. I think I hear voices, but eager to go on, I do not stop. Turning off toward the unmaintained trail that leads down into the Tehipite, I begin my descent. The first part is a gradual slope through rich forests of fir and pine. The lack of wear tells me that the trail is not much traveled, but I notice two sets of footprints coming up out of the valley that is my destination.

At the rim of the canyon, I catch my first glimpse of the Tehipite, and pause in wonder. Plunging down a vertical mile, as deep as the Grand Canyon, with the monolith of Tehipite Dome towering above, mists rising from the green depths, and cut by the legendary Middle Fork Kings River, it recalls romantic images of Yosemite before the tourists had come. The beauty of the place brings tears to my eyes.

I stride down into the Tehipite, confidently navigating the steep unkempt path that switchbacks down, down, down into the beauty I have seen below me. Deciduous leaves litter the ill-marked trail, and I am startled to see thickets of poison oak, rare at that elevation, on all sides of me.

I have temporarily lost the trail, but I am not worried. I know that I will find it again soon. I don't like to be off trail, considering it an unnecessary risk when hiking alone. If anything should happen that might affect my mobility — a twisted ankle, for instance — I prefer to be close to a thoroughfare, where someone would soon come by.

Favoring the seldom-traveled trails that tend to be more loosely marked, I have occasionally lost my way. I enjoy the less trodden areas, finding them to be in keeping with my desires for a wilderness experience, untrampled, infrequently used, not scarred by heavy human footprints or littered with careless debris. I have happened upon some lovely undiscovered spots in just this way. Capable with a compass and a map, I have always been able to find my trail again.

Recent rains have rendered my indistinct path even less visible, and now I have lost my trail into the Tehipite. Alert for signs of the correct route, I am still not especially concerned. I have already drifted off course several times this afternoon, and found my way again. All I have to do is to continue to zigzag carefully down the mountain, and eventually I will find my trail. It is a simple plan, and one that should succeed.

I take one more step, one in hundreds of uneventful steps, and suddenly I am falling through the air. With that one step, everything changes.

7

In the Ravine

The late afternoon sun is sinking rapidly past the edges of the deep ravine where I have fallen, casting it into shadow. The floor of the cleft is perhaps thirty feet across at the place where I am lying. It is cut in the middle by a rippling mountain stream of the sort common in the Sierra: tumbling sometimes over boulders but now running smoothly across the solid, hard face of the rock where I have crash-landed. Ice cold, as snow-fed streams will be, it is perhaps two feet wide where it runs past me, and a few inches deep. The walls of the ravine are steep, made of crumbling rock, well littered with fallen leaves; deciduous and evergreen trees claim precarious outcroppings. The rock is predominantly dark gray, sometimes boasting a reddish cast. The shapes formed by its decomposition make it appear loosely stacked, like handfuls of building blocks thrown on top of each other, to create the walls. It is a beautiful place: moist and fecund with multitudes of tones of green, the last sunlight still illuminating the highest of the leaves, and the rippling brook babbling happily as its sounds echo across the ravine. Usually I love the lengthening shadows, the golden glitter of the late sunshine, and the afternoon bird calls, all preparing for the gentle closing of the day. Today I care little about any of this.

Reeling from the shock of the fall, and astounded to find myself alive, I prop myself into a sitting position. My exploration of the damage continues. I ignore the gaping wound that used to be a knee, the broken nose, and the snapped-off tooth for now. I fight down encroaching awareness of intolerable pain and continue my assessment. Careful prodding indicates no harm to my skull. My internal organs seem intact. I have no apparent spinal injuries. My arms are not broken. The delicate bones of my hands are still functional. I am lucky.

I use my hands to pick up my limp legs and drag them out of the small stream. My clothing is soaked from the splash of the icy water. My heavy hiking boots, which provided support and protection on the trail, are now shoving my feet into painful positions. Clumsily I unlace them and pry them carefully off of each foot. I can still wiggle my toes a little. That's a good sign, I recall: my spine is not severed. Wincing in agony whenever I jolt my left hip, I postulate that it is dislocated and will somehow pop back into alignment. I do not find out until much later that I have broken it in several places.

My backpack has become detached from my body during the fall, and it lies a few feet behind me. Another blessing. I strain backward to reach it and pull it toward me, knowing that with my gear, I have a chance of surviving. Without it, I will die of hypothermia within hours.

Reaching into my pack, I extract my first aid kit, sufficient for a few cuts and mosquito bites but pathetically inadequate for injuries such as mine. Concerned about infection, I empty a small bottle of hydrogen peroxide over the open wound that is my mangled right knee. There is no question of splinting. I don't know which bones are sticking out, or where they would normally go.

Next, I must staunch the blood flow. I have a silk sarong that I always carry with me. It serves as a wrap while I am washing every-thing else, as a headband or neck scarf for warmth, a pot holder or a sun shield for my neck. A gaudy scarf, it is about twenty inches wide by thirty-six inches long, dyed in India in vivid greens and blues and purples. Now I reach for my sarong, and wrap the knee twice around and tie it as tightly as I dare, stopping the bleeding with pressure. Terrified of bumping the mutilated knee and doing even more damage, I next pad it with every bit of extra clothing I have—long pants, a pair of socks and fleece mittens—and tie the whole bundle tightly with my silk long-underwear bottoms.

I dot antibiotic ointment on the more obvious cuts, and apply a rough bandage to the oozing scrape running down my right thigh. There is nothing more that I can do for my injuries.

I cry out a few times, stretching my voice into the woods around me, calling for help that does not come. My voice echoes in the emptiness. There is nobody there to hear me.

Ignoring the stiffness of painful fingers, I grope for my fleece hat and put it on. Wincing with each motion, I pull my long underwear top, insulated vest, and windbreaker over my soggy tank top.

Shaking uncontrollably, I realize I am going into shock. Hot liquids will help. Reaching again into my pack, I haul out my bear canister. It is a cylinder of hard black plastic topped by a lid with two swivel latches, normally easy to open with the twist of a coin, but now a tricky operation. With trembling hands, I manage to get the top off and dig around inside.

Chicken soup is what my mom had prescribed for injuries large and small. I remember her warmth and certainty. I think of the way she used to rub my legs through long nights when they ached with growing pains. I recall her gentle voice, how she seemed to have a way to make any hurt feel better. I remove a packet of powdered soup and screw my little stove onto my can of fuel, lighting the flame with a match barely clutched in painful quivering fingers. Three women I had encountered days ago on the Muir Trail had given the soup to me. I remember our meeting with gratitude. Minutes later, I gulp down a cup of almost reconstituted broth, pull my sleeping bag over me, and pass into merciful unconsciousness.

I don't worry much about what comes next.

"I'll think about that tomorrow," echoes the refrain of the redoubtable heroine of 'Gone with the Wind'. Scarlett could make it through anything, and so can I.

8

A Dozen Ways to Die

E ven as I recoil from the specter of my own death, I find appeal in the concept of dying here in these mountains. No long, slow decay in some cold hospital room for me. No sterile, sealed coffin. My last visions will be of beauty. My bones will crumble to dust and my spirit will be set free to roam hidden canyons and high peaks. I will be united forever with the places that I love, a contribution to the integral balance of the natural world. Vultures will devour my carcass and thrive. My flesh will become fodder for small animals, or perhaps for the magnificent large predators, cougars and mountain lions and bears, who still hide in forgotten places. My bones will mingle with decaying leaves and provide sustenance for growing things. My death will contribute to new cycles of life. I inhale the scent of moist, loamy peat and imagine myself melting into it, becoming part of the earth. My blood calls to these hills.

I know it isn't likely that I'll make it out of the ravine alive. I don't let that drag me into despair, but I do think a lot about how I might succumb.

I have a particular fear of dying of dehydration. Having read accounts of people who expired from lack of water, it is, to my mind, one of the worst ways to go. I would experience extreme thirst, nausea, muscle cramping and headaches. I'd be dizzy, confused and nauseous. My mouth would be dry, tongue swollen and blackened, secretions ceasing and mucus membranes shriveling up. I'd go into a coma and as my blood flow thickened, my heart and kidneys would cease to function.

Fortunately, I have fallen next to a gurgling mountain brook that will provide all the moisture I need as long as I stay close by. It is essential that I not leave the life-giving stream. Disabled as I am, I could not have reached a water source had there not been one nearby. Again I consider how lucky I have been.

I carry a pump through which I filter my drinking water when hiking, wary of the dangers of ingesting protozoa and bacteria from impure water sources. I've had giardia once, a persistent intestinal parasite that caused my stomach to swell up like a balloon. I couldn't eat anything but mashed potatoes for weeks, and the cure had required the extensive ingestion of Flagyl an antibiotic drug. I do not want to get giardia again. Now, however, I am too weak to expend time and energy filtering water. I determine to drink unpurified water from the stream, as much as I can, thirsty or not. It will be essential to prevent dehydration. I will worry about parasites if I get out alive.

The consideration of water brings up the possibility of flooding. There has been an incredible amount of unseasonable rain in the Sierra this year. It has rained every single day of my two-week trip. There has been thunder and lightning, hail, continued drizzling, and, most fearful to me now, gushing downpours that rapidly distend quiet streams to many times their previous depth. A few days ago, I took a break next to one such stream during a sudden rain. By the time the downpour had stopped an hour later, the quiet brook had become a raging torrent, impassible, and swollen to four times its original size.

The ravine in which I lie ranges from twenty to forty feet across, with steep walls on either side. I will have no hope of escaping rapidly rising water or a flash flood if it should rain here or in the higher elevations. I would surely be swept downstream, my body bouncing along the rocks, head sucked under as I am carried to some final resting place. Nothing I can do about that worry, so I put it aside.

Being crushed by a rockslide or knocked out by falling rocks are in the same category. I now understand the volatility of the steep ravine walls. Delicately balanced on one another, the rocks are ready to come tumbling down at any instigation. The sparse shrubbery adorning the rock outcroppings does nothing to ensure the cohesion of the treacherous walls. Rocks the size of my head, strewn about the floor of the ravine, demonstrate the hazard. With such limited ambulatory ability, I cannot move myself out of danger. I simply hope not to be hit by a falling rock.

I consider the threat of hypothermia. It drops to about forty degrees at night, maybe lower. In my weakened condition, I dare not let my core temperature plummet. Under these circumstances, I could die of cold. I am wearing the shorts and tank top that I had been hiking in. I cannot lever myself off the ground enough to change the shorts or to put on long pants, but I can layer up the upper part of my body at night. I also have my down mummy bag. When zipped up, it is sufficient to temperatures of fifteen degrees, as long as I keep it dry. I cannot lift my legs enough to get myself into my bag, so I settle for pulling it over my bare legs, tucking it around me as best as I am able. I have a waterproof tarp that I can draw over me in case of light rain. If I can hang on to my gear, and manage to keep it reasonably dry, it will prevent me from expiring of cold. I will not be comfortably warm, but at least I won't die from the numbing nighttime chill.

I think of starvation. About five days worth of food is left in my bear canister. I look around, eyeing the pine needles speculatively. I don't know much about native plants. Foraging is not encouraged in the national parks. Surely there is something around here I can eat if necessary.

An average-size person, I stand five foot ten and weigh about 140 to 145 pounds. I have seen pictures of people dying of anorexia, the inmates of POW camps, and the victims of famine in less fortunate countries. They were emaciated, weighing perhaps seventy pounds or even less. I have a long way to go before I reach that point. I figure I can last a few months before I actually die of starvation. I'm not hungry anyway.

Loss of blood is an immediate possibility. I have wrapped the only large, open wound, tightly to staunch the blood flow, and it seems to have worked. My makeshift bandage is encrusted with dried blood, but the ooze seems to have slowed. When I am eventually rescued, I will be found to be several pints low, but at the moment, I am content that most of the bleeding has stopped.

The chance of blood poisoning is of more concern. One friend tells a spine-chilling story of a minor cut resulting in shooting red veins requiring emergency hospitalization. I watch my right thigh anxiously for signs of the telltale red lines, knowing that if I see them, I will have to tourniquet my right leg tightly, perhaps saving my life, but almost certainly losing the limb. Do I still want to live if I lose my leg?

I wonder about gangrene, indicated by severe pain and swelling, numbness, and discoloration of the tissue. I certainly have all of those symptoms, but hopefully it is too soon for cellular damage to start to occur. Postulating that I might lose both legs if I stay wounded in the wilderness for long, I ask the question:

"Would I want to live under those circumstances?" The specter of amputation is not a pretty one.

I don't concern myself about rattlesnakes or bears. Those particular dangers seem ridiculously pedestrian in the face of my disaster. Rattlesnakes rarely approach humans, and I won't be stepping on slumbering reptiles any time soon. Occasionally I see bears in my travels, but I am careful to store my food safely, and they have never bothered me. The black bears of the area are largely herbivorous, and in a remote place like the Tehipite, they are generally too shy to approach people. The possible annoyances of bears and rattlesnakes are something I accept every time I set out on a backcountry trek. The potential dangers from the common native fauna pale in comparison to more desperate concerns.

Fortunately, I don't think about coyotes. Someone suggests later that in my weakened condition I could have become bait for bands of

Original "Help me" note written by Amy in the ravine.

coyotes that usually would not attack humans. I do not like to think about being ripped apart by a pack of wild dogs.

The greatest probability is that of dying of infection: becoming feverish and eventually slipping into delirium, unable to care for myself, and falling into a coma. I scrawl a note that I can attach to my body. There is still a chance that I will be found after I pass into unconsciousness.

"I am Amy Racina. Please help me! I broke my legs. Please call..." I write. I give three phone numbers, two for friends, Carla and Adrian, and one for my ex-husband, Big Sam.

I figure I have about three weeks before pervasive infection will get me. As I find out later, I had much less time. During my stay in the ravine, I am blessedly unaware of the imminent danger of systemic bacterial invasion.

Will my family and friends figure out what had happened to me? Probably not. They know only my approximate location. I had made it a point to chat with people on the trail when I encountered them, and tell them where I was headed. Other hikers might remember me, but nobody knows exactly where I am now. It is unlikely that I will be found by chance. People will assume that I had gotten hurt and been unable to reach aid. It happened to a park ranger near Mineral King just a few years ago. I remember seeing signs pleading for information concerning his whereabouts. They never did find his bones.

I imagine my own bones, found perhaps years hence, telling the sad tale of my unfortunate ending. Some chance hiker would stumble upon them, bleached by the sun and picked clean by vultures. Animals would have made off with the smaller bits. Shreds of my gear might still remain. The fillings in my teeth could provide clues. Scientists would study my remains, identify the fractures, and come up with a probable cause of death. They might even be able to find out who I had been.

9

Talking to God

An equal-opportunity spiritualist, I issue my prayers to whatever or whoever should care to heed them and provide help. I acknowledge the existence of God, but God appears to me in many forms. Sometimes I know a male God, sometimes female, sometimes in a clear shape, occasionally as a multitude, and at other times as a voice in my head or an ethereal sense of feeling.

One of my favorite diversions is to travel. I feel a need to absent myself from accustomed situations, to go without that which is familiar, to be open to new influences. The more I see, the more I am capable of seeing. My mind hungers for knowledge, my imagination for new sights and sounds, my spirit for enlightenment.

I don't particularly care where or when I go. The journey is important, not the destination. Comforted by motion as many are soothed by stillness, I like to hoof it about the streets of some new country with my backpack, taking public transit, eating street food, figuring out where to stay, what the local customs are, how best to blend in. What fascinates me is the process of learning, absorbing information as I go along. I often travel on my own, but as with backpacking, I am rarely lonely when on the move. I am so engaged in the delight of discovery that little seems lacking in my life at these times.

One year I got an All-Asia pass from Cathay Pacific; I could visit as many countries in Asia as I could reach in a month. I took myself by train through Thailand, marveled at the reckless pace of Hong Kong, investigated North Korea, tromped all over Singapore, and explored

Malaysia. Every few days I arrived in a new country, fed by the delight and challenge of new sights, new people and newly expanded perceptions.

One of my best-loved pastimes when I travel is to go to various places of worship, quiet my mind, and pray to whatever spirits inhabit these sacred spaces. A two-and-a-half-year course of study at the Berkeley Psychic Institute has given me access to the spirit world. At times, intangible beings seem as real to me as people walking down the street, and I trust in my communication with them. I have prayed in Catholic cathedrals, Episcopal churches, Shaker meetinghouses, Greek temples, Pagan fire circles, Buddhist Wats, and also in the wilderness places that seem especially holy to me. I have been blessed to receive healings and messages from God, from Buddha, from Zeus, from Jesus Christ, from the fiery goddess Pele, from the ancient goddess Inanna, from Aphrodite, and from the Virgin Mary. Angels and spirit guides of varying demeanors have offered help, protection, and guidance. My form of prayer is meditation, often with some type of intention: sometimes simply to seek knowledge or ask for a blessing, general or specific.

In 2002, I was suffering from depression, triggered by the demise of a failed relationship. When I had finally pulled myself out of the limpness of despair, I took a trip to Cambodia. Travel was one of the few things that reliably drew me outside of myself and lifted the grim haze of misery. I went to Phnom Penh, usually used as a jumping off point for the highly touristed Angkor Wat. Ignoring the popular site, I chose instead to wander the streets of the war-torn city. Never had I felt so much suffering and so much endurance of human spirit. Drawn to Wat Phnom, the temple commemorating the spot for which the city was named, I sat down on the floor and closed my eyes to meditate, deeply touched by my sense of the place. Soon I felt the ubiquitous and benevolent presence that I knew as the spirit of the Buddha.

I prayed for understanding.

"Why must I suffer? Why?" The response was immediate. I was engulfed by a perception so vast that I felt my self dissolve. I also felt a very personal touch. "For you, it is an opportunity. So that you may feel greater compassion." Tears rolled down my face. I felt immeasurably blessed. The Buddha himself had touched my mind. My suffering was not needless pain. It was not for nothing.

In later years, I did not chafe against the suffering that was mine. I did not embrace it, but in some way that went beyond words, I understood, and accepted, the nature of suffering.

Now, from my perch in the ravine, I need additional wisdom. I have lost the illusion of human control. I need help from someone or something more powerful than I. I pray in a very human way for my life to be spared.

"Please let me live. Please help me," I pray. Sometimes I have been gifted with what I consider to be miracles, through a prayer, a wish, or simply through an act of fate. Whatever the instigation, I never consider these times to be random, and I am profoundly grateful. On other occasions, praying desperately for some cause whose outcome I deeply desired, I have felt that my wishes are not considered. Consequently I do not feel that divine intervention will necessarily match what I believe to be my own deepest desire. I may die anyway. I do not believe that prayer is a sure thing, but I feel that it might help in some way.

I do not try and make a deal with God. In my experience, that sort of thing doesn't work. Maybe it's that I just don't think of it. Possibly it's because I feel that I'm already doing the best that I can, that my life is already in service to whatever powers have put me here. Or perhaps I need to admit my own helplessness. I don't try and negotiate a bargain, but I do ask for help.

In response to my prayers, I am not surprised to feel the compassionate wisdom and gentle irony that I associate with my dealings with the divine. Nor am I astonished to hear that whether I live or die ultimately does not matter, that praying for my own life is pointless. The message is delivered with infinite understanding and gentle but inarguable truth. I am led to remember that eventually all humankind will die. It is our fate. In the great scheme of things, death of the human form is a certainty. Only the exact timing of my death is in question, and when held against the measure of the inevitable, and the timelessness of eternity, that is not important. I understand the irony of my plea. I am oddly comforted by the response.

I feel the quality of the sacred in the very desperation of my situation. Poised between life and death, I teeter on the knife's edge of my own existence. Whatever happens, whether I go or whether I stay, the waves from this decision will cast reverberations through the lives of many, touching a fate much greater than that of one lone woman, echoing long past that one step and this one prayer. My being comes sharply into focus in the crystalline clarity of this moment in time. What will the fates decide?

I still want to live. I pray on. There is another message for me, seemingly contradictory, but inarguable as well. I am familiar with messages from God that appear to be paradoxical. There are truths that are greater than right or wrong, more complex than the limited inclinations of the human mind can encompass. And so I listen as well to the next message:

"How much you want to live is what will make a difference." I realize that I have been brought to this juncture so that I may study the life that I have almost lost and might still lose. Offered the unique opportunity to look carefully at the life that I inhabit, I have the chance to decide definitively. How much do I want to live?

I have a good life. Born into a privileged race, onto an affluent continent, I have always had enough food to eat, education available to me, leisure to do as I wish much of the time. I have managed to attain most of my goals, to acquire many of the things that I want. I am healthy, strong and intelligent. I have adequate income, good friends, a nice middle class place to live, and a beautiful teenage son. I have traveled enough to have seen lives of people who are less fortunate, and I know how lucky I am.

I have a fairly comfortable existence by most standards, but like many who were born to relative luxury, I can still find fault. Weather is lousy, I am grumpy, and traffic is bad. There is always too much to do. True love often seems to elude me. Small complaints are allowed to dominate, and I waste hours or days griping about trifling imperfections. Too many moments have been misspent by not acknowledging the value of life.

I am also haunted by dim memories of a better and brighter place and time, of a world where everything was wonderful and easy and filled with the light of love. I do not know where or what this place is, but I know it well. Sometimes these memories seem so vivid to me that I weigh the turmoil of everyday life on the planet earth against them, and find it sadly lacking. I have lingering feelings that I've been dropped off in some unfortunate place, dumped by mistake in a hostile environment, that I am being punished, for some unknown infraction, by my visit to this lifetime.

Sometimes I have experienced ambivalence. Is life a good thing? Is it worth going on? Now, faced with the ultimate question: "How much do you care to live?" I find that I do, very much, want to live. There is no doubt whatsoever. Despite my understanding that there are no guarantees, I determine to do whatever I can to make life the probable outcome. I want to live. That sweet swift moment of total assurance becomes a treasure in my memory, because for one glowing second, I experience absolutely no ambivalence. My decision is made.

In the coming months, I would often refer back to that moment of clarity. Days were sometimes bad, life was hard, and people and circumstances were annoying. But never did I stray far from that choice.

I want to live.

10

The Go-Lite Girl

Introduced to backpacking by my dad, with his minimalist
approach, I have never seen the sense in hauling a heavy load. I
have always carried less than many, but even so, sometime in my
forties I noticed that my knees had begun to ache unpleasantly after
prolonged hiking journeys.

About this time, I came across the work of Ray Jardine, well-trav-
eled go-light backing guru, adventure enthusiast and author of *Beyond
Backpacking: Ray Jardine's Guide to Lightweight Backpacking.* I read the
volume with great interest, enjoying the exploits of Ray and his wife
Jenny.

Ray believes in taking as little as possible and in making personal
choices. Decide for yourself what you want to schlep and what you
can do without. He expounds upon the toll that a few extra pounds of
unnecessary equipment can take on the legs and on the trip, and offers
up suggestions for making one's own lightweight items.

Inspired by the book's practical, yet delightfully irreverent approach
to my favorite sport, I set out to lighten up my own pack. For several
years, I carefully weigh each and every item, trimming the handle off
the toothbrush, cutting my foam mattress down to a mere eighteen by
twenty-four inches, chopping my bandana in half, snipping tags and
extra features off of my gear. I scrutinize each item, falling for replace-
ments only if they are both lighter and more functional than what I
already have. I can be seen at thrift stores and outdoor supply shops
carrying my portable scale, the better to weigh potential purchases.

Obsessively I track down the lightest of the light titanium tent stakes, silicone tarps, breathable nylon shell pants. If I can't find the gear I want, I make my own.

I think of potential dangers. I decide to continue carrying a water filter to protect against giardia. I elect to take a bear canister to shield my food from unwanted interest. I carry a snakebite kit and a packet of first aid necessities. Packing light means being better prepared, not less so.

I consider desired comforts as well. I jettison much of what others find essential: a towel, a pillow, changes of clothing. I do pack plenty of tea leaves, and a good book. I weigh each paperback, with an eye toward maximal words per ounce, then rip off the cover of the chosen volume. With the reassuring solace of a good book and a hot cup of tea, I have the amenities I need.

I plan to use each piece of equipment for several purposes. My tarp serves as a tent, a pack cover, or a poncho. Extra clothing in a stuff sack makes a comfy pillow. Two other stuff sacks double as camp booties. A homemade water carrier turns into a wash bucket or sink. A trekking pole becomes a tent pole. My silk sarong provides service as a warm scarf, a sun shield, an extra outfit, and a potholder.

I buy myself a GoLite "Gust" backpack, its weight just one pound, four ounces. It has no frame, and looks a bit like a large garbage bag strapped to my back. I find that when properly packed, the clever design provides its own shaping, along with an extremely comfortable ride on rugged trails. I rapidly bond with my pack, and refuse to hike with anything else. I put 900 miles on it.

I also invest in a cushy ultralight sleeping bag. The Mountainsmith "Vision" is the bag of my desire, a luxurious cloud of premium goose down nestled into a featherweight shell of an incandescent silvery color. Guaranteed to keep me snug in temperatures down to fifteen degrees, and weighing just one pound, fifteen ounces, it is everything I've ever wanted in a bag. I pay the pricey $300 without a backward glance, and set off into the woods with my latest acquisition.

It is true love from the first night out. I feel like a princess, toasty warm in a cocoon of fluffy soft down. I cherish that bag, protecting the delicate feathers religiously, taking care not to crush, overwash or otherwise damage them. Perhaps it's a bit much, I think, feeling guilty about the luxurious comfort of my new precious. After all, I rarely see temperatures as cold as fifteen degrees. I reason that if I'm ever hurt, or stranded, I may need that extra warmth.

After a couple of years of refining my choices, my efforts have paid off. This is what I pack for my trip.

Gear Chart   Base Pack Weight

Gear	Weight
GoLite "Gust" Backpack	20 oz.
Mountainsmith "Vision" Sleeping Bag-with stuff sack	31 oz.
Integral Designs Sil Tarp-5 ft.x 8 ft. silicone impregnated nylon	7 oz.
Mosquito net-spider-shaped	5 oz.
Tent stakes-titanium-6 7in.	1.4 oz.
Fork and spoon-lexan	0.5 oz.
Bear canister	44 oz.
Ensolite foam pad-1 ½ by 2 ft.	2 oz.
Pot with lid-titanium	4.8 oz.
Cup-titanium	3.1 oz.
MSR "Pocket Rocket" stove	3.2 oz.
Water filter	15 oz.
Wide-mouth bottle-lexan	4.4 oz.
Bladder-style bottles-2-1 liter and 1.5 liter	3 oz.
Water carrier-made from cut-up gallon plastic bottle	1 oz.
Small stuff sacks-2 (double as camp booties)	3 oz.
Large garbage bags-2	2 oz.
Black Diamond headlamp	0.5 oz.
Small sharp knife	0.5 oz.
Trowel-plastic	2 oz.
Ground cloth-nylon	3 oz.
Maps (edges trimmed off) and itinerary	3 oz.
Writing paper, 2 pens	1.3 oz.
Reading glasses-2 pr.	2.8 oz.

Small silk bag with extras:

waterproof-windproof matches, regular strike-anywhere matches, sewing kit, duct tape, 2 safety pins, 30 ft. of nylon cord .... 4.6 oz.

Small silk bag with cosmetics and first aid:

biodegradable liquid soap (3 oz.), sunscreen (2 oz.), talcum powder (1 oz.), A & D ointment (0.5 oz.), toothpaste (1 oz.), toothbrush, dental floss, three packets of antibiotic ointment, two gauze pads, bottle of hydrogen peroxide (2 oz.), eight Band-Aid adhesive bandages, Moleskin adhesive bandages, Chap Stick lip balm, snakebite extractor, fourteen ibuprofen, plastic backpacking mirror, half a small comb .... 9 oz.

Gear Base Weight .... **174.1 oz.**

Clothing	Weight
Breathable nylon shell jacket	7 oz.
Breathable nylon shell pants	5 oz.
Silk long underwear tops and bottoms	6 oz.
Insulated vest	4 oz.
Pair of thick ragg socks	3.3 oz.
Pair of liner socks	1.8 oz.
Fleece hat (homemade)	2 oz.
Fleece mittens (homemade)	1.2 oz.
Head cover mosquito net	0.4 oz.
Half a cotton bandana	0.3 oz.
Silk sarong	1.5 oz.
Two-piece swimsuit	5 oz.
One pair underwear	1.2 oz.
Clothing Base Weight	**38.7 oz.**
Base pack weight for gear and clothing totals	**212.8 oz.**
	(13 lb. 4.8 oz.)

I add consumables, items that will be used up as I go along. Those vary depending on the length of the excursion. For this trip, my food weighs seventeen pounds. Calculated at maximal calories per ounce (about 150) that gives me 2,400 calories a day to hike on. I take two canisters of fuel at one-pound, ten ounces and a paperback book that weighs fourteen ounces, for a total of nineteen pounds, eight ounces for the consumables.

Adding base pack weight to the consumables, this means that I leave the trailhead for this trip with a little under thirty-three pounds on my back.

I wear sturdy leather hiking boots, a pair of liner socks, a pair of Ragg Wool socks, underwear, shorts, a bra, a tank top, and a men's silk long-sleeved shirt. My favorite hiking shirt is a faded chartreuse silk, bought for fifty cents at the Salvation Army. I wear a hat, and carry a single trekking pole.

Now, crippled in the ravine, I see that my pack has mercifully fallen within reach. It is light enough that I can pull it toward me. I hug my pack to me. It has been a cherished companion, and just now, it seems to me to be my only friend. Immobilized and badly injured, without my gear, I would have had no chance at all. I give thanks for every hour I have spent obsessing over each piece of equipment. I have what I need to give me a chance at survival. I have hot tea to comfort me. I even have a book to read.

11

The First Day

fter a restless night of drifting in and out of sleep, plagued by disturbing dreams that I cannot quite remember, trying uselessly to avoid the throbbing aches from my battered body, I struggle again into consciousness. There is no relief with the morning light. The nightmare goes on. I find myself draped uncomfortably over a cold, bloodstained rock, clothing still sodden from sweat and stream water, sleeping bag clutched over my shivering body, bits of gear strewn about me.

On most days, I love the hours before dawn. The mornings are the best of times, full of promise and the joy of hours yet unknown. I am rested from the night's sleep, the world is sparkling, a new adventure awaits. Soon the sun will illuminate the landscape, and stray tentacles will find me through the trees and warm my body and dry out my gear, moist and glistening from the night's frost.

This particular morning is different. I am just glad the long night is over. I have tugged my little piece of mattress partially under my back, but I am unable to roll over onto either side or otherwise adjust my position for more comfort. I have a boot under my head as a pillow, having used my extra clothing to pad my wounded knee.

A quick check of my little compass/thermometer shows thirty-eight degrees, just a bit above freezing. Brrr. My clock reads 5:35. I struggle to a sitting position and make preparations for my day. I dare not think too carefully about the extent of my injuries or about my chances for survival. There are discomforts to be overcome, plans to be made. It's just another day in the wilderness.

Comforted by the routine, I do first what I always do in the morning. Pulling my bear canister into range, I grope for my instant coffee and put a pot of water onto my stove to heat. Gently shaking my red fuel can, I estimate that I have about six days of fuel left if I am thrifty. That means boiling two cups of water for breakfast and two cups for dinner, one for tea or coffee and one for food.

I have to pee. I can think of no civilized way to accomplish this. I can't stand up; I can't push myself up off the ground. I can't pull my clothing down. I settle for just peeing in my clothes, pulling my bedding away first, and feeling the warm flow as I let go of lingering inhibitions and refined habits. I feel the warm wet urine soak my clothes, then trickle away, steaming in the chill air. I stare at the moist rivulets, making their way down the rock. The pressure on my bladder has been relieved and I am grateful. Another problem solved. How little it takes for me to feel satisfaction.

I don't bother to redress my wounds. I used up all of my antibiotic ointment and disinfectant the day before. I have no more bandages or clean cloths of any sort. I cringe at the thought of looking again at my own mangled flesh, so I do not unwrap my knee. I look anxiously at what I can see of my legs. They are swollen a nasty pinkish color, but there are no red shooting veins. Nor is there an unhealthy greenish tinge to the flesh. I am thankful for that.

It is chilly enough that I covet the heat from my scalding coffee. The small pleasure of hot liquid running down my throat brings brief respite from the pain of my situation. I focus on the comfort, holding my cup closely, both hands wrapped around the warm titanium.

Generally I am a goal-oriented person. I prefer to be doing something, to have some aim, some purpose. I usually have a course of action in mind. Sometimes I have been criticized for these tendencies. I should be content to just be, not to do, to live in the moment, to simply wait and see what will unfold, be more receptive, more passive, less attached, I am told. Now, I give no thought to analyzing or modifying my behavior. I do what comes naturally to me. I make a plan.

In this situation, I know that it is unacceptable to me to merely sit and wait. That would most likely be signing my death warrant. I might not be found until too late. Lying here and thinking about dying, rumi-

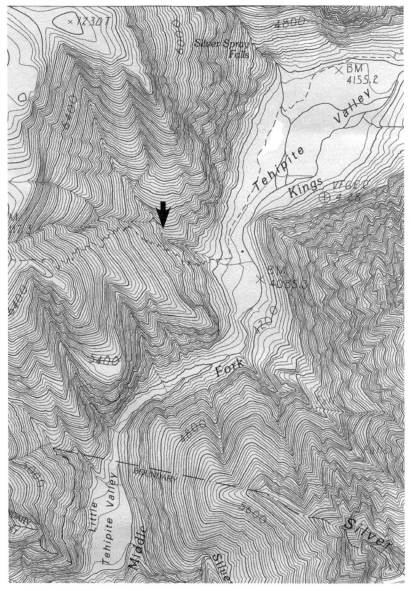

Blow up of topo map showing exact location of fall.

nating on my own pain, wondering which nasty slide into death will become my fated passage, is intolerable. Besides, I want to live.

My best chance for survival is to get to a trail. Rangers have told me that only a few people hike in this area each season, but I myself have met three in the past week, and followed the footprints of two more. That means that a handful of hikers have hiked the trails in this area in the past two weeks: those odds of rescue are somewhat better. I resolve to call out occasionally in the unlikely possibility that someone should be passing by. If I can get to a traveled path, there is at least some chance that I will be found before time runs out. Even if I should go unconscious and be unable to cry out for help, I may yet be saved. But where is the trail? Where am I?

I have no idea where the pathway that I had lost the previous day might be. My best guess is that it is somewhere up above where I now lie. I eye the narrow gorge into which I have fallen. The steep, cliff-like hillsides climbing up several hundred feet are clearly inaccessible to me in my current state. I still cannot move my legs. Finding yesterday's trail is out of the question.

The floor of the ravine tilts downhill, sometimes almost level, sometimes dropping steeply. The trickling stream flows happily away, guided by the sloping rock toward unseen meanderings below. My eyes follow the flowing water as I gaze longingly down the ravine, straining to see past trees and bushes that obscure my view.

Somewhere down there, I know from my map, is another trail. The route I have lost eventually intersects a slightly larger path that runs the length of the Tehipite Valley. Somewhere down the ravine, my little creek will flow into the Middle Fork Kings River. Next to the river is the larger trail. If I can somehow drag myself to that trail and lay myself across it, I will have a chance of being found. Willing myself to take hope and determined to have a plan, I seize upon this improbable possibility.

I try to estimate how far down into the Tehipite I hiked before I fell. It had been getting late in the afternoon, and I believe myself to be about four-fifths of the way down, maybe more. If I am right, I have about 1,000 feet of elevation drop before I get to the river. That means that I will have to drag myself anywhere from three-fourths of a mile to two miles, assuming I can get through. I may be able to inch my way down the slope of the ravine. I can only see about thirty yards ahead of me. Beyond that, my view is blocked by a turn in the creek and a small cluster of trees and rocks. But this first part looks passable. No ugly drops or daunting barriers. As I peer downward through the trees, I fancy that I see a brightening that implies an opening in the vegetation, perhaps the meadow at the bottom of the valley. Holding tight to this grain of hope, I organize myself for the journey.

By moving, I will be adding to my burden of pain, and possibly increasing the extent of my injuries. I ignore both these likelihoods. Immobilization is a luxury that I cannot afford. If I die, to have saved myself from additional pain and injury will be unimportant.

In the spot where I sit, the ravine slopes perhaps thirty to thirty-five degrees. During the night, I have already slipped down a foot or two. Gravity will assist me in my trek, and I can amplify my body's inclination to slide down the ravine by using my hands. Pushing up with my arms, ignoring their minimal injuries, I find that I cannot lift my butt so much as a few inches off the ground, but that I can shove myself along, facing forward, in a sitting position. I have only my arms to help me. My legs are a dead weight. If I can ease myself into the stream, the small flow of water will help me still further.

Experimentation tells me that I can only scootch down the ravine, not up. The effort of pushing my limp body up the gradual incline is too much for me. Immediately I grow concerned that I will lose my gear, perhaps sliding out of arm's reach, and be unable to reclaim it. Once I start my journey down the ravine, there will be no going back. There will be no question of retrieving anything I have left behind.

A small mistake under these circumstances could cost me my life. Looking about me for items I might have forgotten, I think long and hard about possible uses for my boots. Reluctantly, I decide to abandon them. My feet are far too swollen to put them back on, even if I am able to endure the pain. I won't be standing up anytime soon, and will not need coverings other than socks on my feet. I don't want the additional weight of the heavy boots. Carefully, I extract the laces and tuck them into my pack. I collect up everything else and stow it securely. The loss of any small article could mean the difference between life and death.

I also worry that my equipment, especially my precious sleeping bag, will become saturated if I drag it through the water. Down loses its insulating properties when it gets wet. I need the warmth of my fluffy "Vision" more than ever. I pack my bag into its stuff sack, wrap it in one plastic garbage bag and then another. I think back to the day when a friendly hiker told me where to find two garbage bags under a rock.

I take off all of my warm clothing, packing it also in a torn garbage bag that I hope will be mostly waterproof. I pack my gear into my pack as I usually do, bear canister on the bottom, miscellaneous items in the middle, sleeping bag on top. I tie one end of an eight-foot piece of nylon rope to the shoulder straps of my pack and the other end around my waist, planning to drag it along behind me.

I waste no energy on anything not essential. I don't bother with tooth brushing or hair combing. I can hardly bear to look at my battered face in my little mirror. I don't try to clean anything or even to cook breakfast. I focus instead on the journey ahead of me. I keep a water bottle handy and put a Clif Bar energy bar into the outside pocket of my pack where it will be available for quick energy. I continue wearing the shorts and tank top. Over the tank top I pull my long-sleeved silk shirt, as a barrier from the sun. With a hat to shield my head, and soggy hiking socks on my feet for protection against the rough rocks, I am ready to go.

By now the sun is touching the bottom of the ravine. I choose a goal that is about ten yards away. The smooth face of the ravine bottom changes at that point. The stream drops into a little pool, hemmed in by a large rock on the right and scrubby trees on the left. Inch by inch, I head for that pool. Scootching myself along, digging my fingers into rock outcroppings and shoving my inert lower body forward with trembling arms, I perfect my technique and learn my limitations. My right knee is effectively immobilized in a semi-bent position by its own swelling and the bundle of clothing I wrapped around it the night before. Terrified of injuring it still further, I try not to allow the knee to flex at all. I have to keep my left hip from tilting from side to side, or waves of pain overwhelm and stop me. I inch along a foot or two, then reach back to pull my pack along with me, sacrificing my trusty GoLite "Gust" as I rake it brutally across the harsh rock. An hour later, I have reached my goal of ten yards.

Now I have to navigate my way around the first major obstacle. The pool of water is about three feet across and a foot and a half deep. Bordered by a large rock on one side and a scrub of trees on the other, the only way past the pool is through it. Carefully, I ease myself on my butt, feet first, into the pool. The absence of gravity in the water is a slight relief from pain and effort. To get out requires more ingenuity. I must turn myself face down, without putting pressure on the massacred right knee, and lug myself up onto the big rock on my tummy, turning back over before I am completely out of the water, all without aggravating any of my injuries. I struggle to drag myself, belly down, out of the pool, which contributes its suction to counter my efforts. A scream of agony is wrenched from my gut as the left hip tilts perilously. I push with all my failing strength, a twist of the hip engulfing me in waves of pain so intense that I fear I will black out. Propped as I am, partially over the pool, I know that if I pass out, I'll slide down and surely drown. I fight down the pain and lock my trembling arms until it passes. I must not lose consciousness.

The collar of what was once my favorite hiking shirt has snagged on a stick. Skewered and helpless to free myself, I pull until the shirt rips in pieces off my back and I am again free to continue my journey. I feel badly about littering the wilderness with scraps of chartreuse silk, but can think of no way to retrieve the ragged pieces.

Finally I succeed in hauling myself out of the pool with quaking limbs and turning my limp body over onto my back. Beached like a spawning salmon on the large sunny rock, I fall immediately into a sleep of exhaustion.

I awake some time later to find my hat and my pack floating in the little pool, out of my reach. Happily, the backpack is still tied to me. Unable to haul it up to where I am perched, I wrestle a long forked stick out of a tangle of brush behind me, and stretch it toward the pack. By pulling on the stick and the rope with all of my fading strength, I finally retrieve my gear, now soaked through. My hat floats out of reach, teasing me as it bobs merrily. My sleeping bag and extra clothing are still somewhat dry.

I call out for help, as I do periodically, doubting that anyone is about, but wishing blindly that someone might hike by. There is no answer. I still have only myself to rely upon.

Groping for sustenance, I force myself to gulp down some water and half a Clif Bar energy bar. A few bites are all I can manage, but I have to keep my energy level up.

The next couple of hours find me inching downstream, within a narrow channel in the rock carved out by years of abrading water. The water and the ravine head steeply downhill at this point. The channel is several inches deep and about as wide as my body, narrowing in some places to just seven or eight inches. Will I slide out of control, mimicking my previous fall? I dare not think about that, lest my newly acquired fears paralyze my will. I ease my body again into the stream, and scootch myself down the narrow indentation in the rock, shoving my limp legs before me. My body dams the flow; water hits my back and rises up alarmingly on either side of me, but it brings relief from the pain in my legs with its cool rush. Periodically the indentation narrows, and I have to lift one leg or the other out of the crevice with my hands, trying not to tilt onto my injuries, nor get a leg stuck in a rocky crack. I clamp my teeth together. Each inch is an effort; each yard provides a new sequence of challenges for my damaged body and uncertain strength. Entirely engaged in making it through the next few moments, there is no space in my mind for trickling thoughts of fear or regret.

Finally, my exhausted body can go no further. I eat the rest of my snack, a Chocolate Chip Peanut Crunch Clif Bar energy bar. Usually it's a favorite. Now, it tastes like sawdust, but I force it down. I pull out my gear as I check out the spot where I have landed by default. It is less than ideal. I'm huddled under an overhanging ledge, rockfall a definite possibility. Water trickles under me from the ravine wall in a steady cold ooze. Beetles skitter over my recumbent form. The rock on which I lay is convex, and I keep sliding down. There is nowhere flat enough to perch my stove. It doesn't matter. I have reached the end of my strength. I pull my still moist sleeping bag over my soggy clothes, and fall again into unconscious sleep, too tired to worry about what comes next. It has been a grueling day. I have covered about thirty yards.

Pain

There was no pain at the moment of impact. Certainly I felt an agony of mind in the seconds before I crashed to the ground, a fierce desire to live and a desolation at having life snatched away, but as for physical pain, there was nothing.

Months after the fall I am sitting placidly in a hot tub, my eyes closed in a light meditation, when I shudder suddenly with the wrenching terror of blinding physical pain—the palpable feeling of my bones crushing and flesh ripping apart, like a lightning bolt penetrating every cell of my body. Jerking back into consciousness, the memory is gone as swiftly as it has come. Although I am healing well at this point, my body will ache for days afterward, and I'll be convinced that I have re-injured myself. Somewhere, deep in the recesses of my awareness, the instant of intolerable agony was experienced and stored as a subconscious memory. But in the actual millisecond of crashing on the rock, I felt nothing.

Of course there is pain in the aftermath of the fall, in those long days alone in the ravine. I feel the torment of my wrecked body, and fight it down. Or I give voice to my anguish, allowing it to issue forth in long wails that call out for help to any who might hear.

But I cannot let the pain overwhelm me, and I feel separate somehow from the wretched torment of broken limbs and torn flesh. I must not allow physical agony to sabotage my actions, or reduce my chances of survival. I will not let pain take me to unconsciousness while crossing a pool of water, or permit it to cloud my mind before my gear is secure and my food safely stored. I have no extra energy to invest in suffering. There is too much at stake. It is as though I have stepped back from the physical experience, and consider pain solely as a practical problem, almost an intellectual exercise.

In retrospect, the agony should have been unbearable. According to the doctors who treated me later, the pain ought to have been excruciating. I am incredulous as well, as I think back upon the experience. Why was I not aware of the full caliber of the physical devastation?

Perhaps I was simply in a state of shock, too traumatized to engage in complete feeling, my body too badly injured to understand how much it had been hurt. This innate physiological device served as a useful physical tool, the shock and adrenaline staying with me and numbing the brunt of the anguish for the four days and nights that I was stranded in the ravine.

I also credit my spiritual guidance, often a comfort to me in times of physical as well as emotional challenge.

"You will never be given more than you can bear." The message has come to me often, from some place of greater wisdom than I alone possess. Throughout my life, in moments of extreme misery, I have heard these same words, in response to both mental and physical anguish. Though emotional pain is different from bodily pain, the fear is the same. Will I, at some point, be unable to take any more? Will the pain overwhelm me, become more than I can stand? During trying times, I have sometimes felt that I would simply expire of the torment, cease to exist, self-combust. I have not. I have not gone insane, or turned to drugs, or killed myself, or sought whatever other forms of solace might be available to those who simply cannot tolerate their lives as they are. I will never be given more than I can bear. I cling to the words. I try to believe the promise.

It's not that I have never known physical pain. I don't consider myself to be particularly stoic. I wince at sudden bumps and bruises. I demand extra novocaine at the dentist. I complain about sunburn and reach for the aspirin bottle when I have a headache.

My gold standard of pain is the toothache that required an emergency root canal, several years ago. A few hours into the sudden experience found me at the ER of the local hospital, pacing frantically and begging for painkillers. At no time in the ravine was the pain from multiple fractures of both legs as bad as the agony from that one tooth.

When I am at last rescued, and have access to Vicodin painkiller and morphine and the many miracle drugs of modern pain control, I find the entire arsenal to be less powerful than whatever protects me from the awareness of my own misery during these long lonely days and nights. The physical devices and spiritual gifts that have left me unaware of the extremity of the pain are far more effective. The promise has been fulfilled. I have not been given more than I can bear. I am able to survive the pain.

13

Longing for Life

In the few fragile seconds before I crash, I grab a quick glimpse of what I will miss when I die. I see bright colors before my world drops into black and white. I want the colors so badly. I see the pretty clothes that I love to collect, jewel tones of sapphire and ruby and emerald. I have a fleeting vision of the sparkling colors of the Sierra summer, luminous greens and blues and poppy yellows. I don't think so much about the actual people and situations of my life, I want only the colors, their joy and energy and beauty, the technicolor of a life I have discovered too late that I love.

I have an interesting and unconventional life. Rarely am I without a cause to support, a group to organize, an enthusiasm to pursue. Active in local organizations of various sorts, I put many hours into helping organize potlucks and events for WaCCO Singles, a local Sonoma County singles group. I lead hikes and women's groups. I participate in a women's writing group as well. I'm known about my town, as a result of days of Little League and soccer, my son's school connections, and daily trips to the post office. An eager traveler, I am often out exploring, hiking or camping or backpacking. I love to ferret out the best deals on the Internet and travel to foreign countries every couple of months, often by myself, meeting people as I go. I do a bit of dating, but it's been a decade since I've had a satisfactory long-term relationship. Though I live alone with my son, I meet scores of people in an amazing variety of venues.

My work life is also unusual. After being an art director for an advertising agency, then specializing in wine label packaging for about ten years, I became an entrepreneur. I currently have two small businesses. The first, Instant Pool Cards, involves manufacturing and filling orders for one product, a ten-way card with a random number selection under a pull-tab. Sold for entertainment, it is used mostly for football, baseball and hockey pools. My second business is a mobile clothing boutique called The Everyday Goddess. I go about to festivals and fairs and set up my tent to sell fun, flashy, danceable clothing of the genre known in California as "Goddesswear," which I acquire during trips to Asia and other colorful places. I take my store to all sorts of interesting venues, such as workshops, pagan festivals and polyamory events. I love to decorate people. My customers often become my friends.

In the best of times, I love my life and consider it my finest creative effort. I delight in encouraging others to seek new paradigms as well.

In the days that follow my fall, given a reprieve from death, but with survival still not assured, I have the chance to consider the quality of my existence.

Much of what claims my time and concern in everyday life seems irrelevant now. Usually I obsess over taxes unpaid, bank accounts unbalanced, floors unswept. None of the time constraints and responsibilities that I commonly use to measure my own productivity seem to matter at all. The agony of undone chores, unfinished goals and incomplete strivings is forgotten.

I don't criticize my own previous choices. I haven't led a blameless life, but I've always felt that I've done the best that I could. I do not beat myself up now for not accomplishing more, for not influencing enough people, for not impacting the world, for not doing additional good while I was alive. I do not flagellate myself for not fulfilling my purpose. Who knows what that is anyhow? Maybe my destiny is to die here in the wilderness.

I wonder about people with whom I have left things unsaid. I've read enough accounts of near-death experiences to think that I should have regrets about unfinished interactions, situations that are unresolved. I've done a pretty good job, I consider. My loved ones have been told that I love them. I've impacted some people in a positive way, helped some unfortunates, left the world a slightly better place. But there are a few loose ends, a few people that I do not understand, or have not yet forgiven. I have grown apart from my sister. We don't communicate much lately. There are a few lovers from whom I departed in pain and anger.

Touched by a rare clarity of vision in those days between life and death, I realize that none of this matters. It's all OK If I haven't finished everything, cleared things up with everyone, it will be right for me to go or stay regardless. If there are things to be completed, in the vast scheme of destiny, they will come to fruition when the time is ripe. It is not my burden to bear. I am but a ripple in a bigger pond.

I have many friends and acquaintances, but will they mourn me for long? Probably not. All are accustomed to my going off frequently on some jaunt, tromping about Asia for a month here, wandering thru Scotland for a few weeks, heading up into the wilderness. It'll take a while for people to notice I've disappeared. They'll shake their heads a bit, then forget about me, talk about the next news item, and move on with their lives.

I am not certain how much I will be remembered. Not much, I think. I have no partner, no enduring intimate relationships. My parents are long dead. I have a brother living in Olympia, Washington, and a sister whom I seldom see. No, my passing will have little impact on the world.

I think a lot about my son, Sam. He turned sixteen last February, and does a pretty good job of seeming not to need me anymore. I suppose I've modeled independence to him over the years. Always a strong-willed person, from his very early life, I have no doubt of his survival and self-determination. He is already who he will be, and seems less and less interested in whatever slight influence I might wield.

I am sorry, for his sake, that he will lose his mom at so early an age. I figure he'll be a little sad, but I wonder how much he'll really miss me. I'll be leaving him the house, the car, and the cat. He'll go to stay with his dad, no doubt, living just up the highway in the next town.

I care deeply for my son, feeling the things that bring him pain almost more than he does himself. I know him for his sensitive soul and soft heart despite the independent bravado of an adolescent, and I am sorry for what angst he will feel. I want desperately to spare him all of it, for him to have a life filled with happiness and untouched by the emotional agonies that I have felt myself. I have known for some time that I cannot, however much I desire it, spare him his pain or walk his path for him. He has his own life to live. He won't be afraid to pursue his dreams. I've given him that. But he'll have to make it without a mom from here on. He will be OK. He will have to be. Oh Sam, I'm so very sorry.

What I do value is the turbulent delight of a life lived in constant motion, rich with color and knowledge and the vibrancy of new experience. What I regret the most are the lost times of happiness. When I think that I might lose it all, what breaks my heart is that I will not live to feel again the wonderful moments, the sweet connections, the times of joy and awe and celebration. So often in my busy life, I have lost those times in concerns and sadness, in attention to unimportant details. How infinitely precious those bright moments seem to me now.

A lifetime spent on successes and failures, in worry and reward, in tears and laughter and regret and relief, in deep sadness and radiant joy. A lifetime, distilled into a few hours of a few final days. A few hours to know what is ultimately important.

In those lucid hours in the ravine, my life so precious as I watch it fading away, I choose the brightness. What I will miss the most, what makes mine a life worth living are the times of joy, of light and laughter and celebration. I will miss the wonderful places yet to be visited, the victories yet to be experienced, the meals not yet savored, the flowing words unspoken, unread or unwritten, the lovely people I will never meet. That is what I will miss, those lost moments are what I regret. Unapologetically, relentlessly selfish, I want to live. I want to live for myself, and for all the joy that I might never have again.

It is the colors that I crave. I can see them slipping away and my soul weeps at the loss.

14

The Second Day

I awake before dawn, stiff and uncomfortable. Unable to go back to sleep, although my clock reads just 3:45, I wait for daybreak to arrive. While I wait, I use my flashlight to read. I remember that day at the Muir Trail Ranch, when the kind old woman had dug the little light out of a stack of odds and ends and given it to me.

I am reading a tattered paperback edition of Gary Jennings' *Aztec*, a historical novel recreating with vivid detail the colorful existence of long-gone Aztec cultures. Life was rough then. The characters in the book are often to be found clambering through the woods with mangled limbs and disfiguring diseases. For two weeks now I have been reading *Aztec*, and by this time I have become somewhat immune to gory descriptions of deliberate mutilation and accidental dismemberment. By comparison to the life of the Aztecs, my own situation seems, if not commonplace, at least acceptable. I ration the 1,038 pages like I ration my food supplies. I have about 380 pages left.

I know that I dare not ease myself back into the stream, soaking myself in icy water, until the sun ventures again into the depths of my ravine. I will need the midday heat. My overtaxed body cannot be trusted to warm itself. I am still chilly from dragging myself through the water the day before, clothing still damp. I know from yesterday's journey that my window of warmth will be narrow. I will have just two or three hours of sunshine before being left again in shadow.

Planning to continue down the ravine, I eye my route for the day like the obstacle course that it is. Each rock and stick represents a potentially insurmountable barrier. Each tilt in the landscape means painful reorganization of my body. I have a greater appreciation now of how difficult each yard will be, but I am coming to know the limitations of my wounded body and what to expect from each movement. I must go on.

My swollen feet are still encased in the same soggy wool hiking socks I was wearing when I fell, hopefully providing at least some insulating warmth. My feet are too numb for me to tell, though I can still move my toes, only slightly. I have no long-sleeved shirt to wear this morning. Its ripped pieces still decorate yesterday's path. Happily, the hat that had floated out of reach has drifted closer in the night, and I am able to nab it with a stick, wet but intact. Again, I tie my pack to my waist with its rope.

When the sun finally creeps into my ravine, I am ready. I inch my way down off of the large rock that has been my perch overnight. The rock is clammy and sloping. The cliff above me looks ready to give way at any moment. I am glad to leave the unwelcoming spot.

My first obstacle is a long narrow channel like the one I faced yesterday. The icy water comes once more as a shock, shoving at me with its strength. I fight constantly, having only the use of my arms to keep myself from slipping out of control. Am I growing weaker? I plan carefully, focusing on each move, anxious to avoid getting a foot or my torso wedged in a groove against a rock, and being unable to extricate it. I must make no mistakes. My body no longer works in the ways I am accustomed to.

The difficult task before me keeps my mind constantly engaged. I do not have the leisure to fall into despair or to give in to pain. There is a job to be done, and it requires all of my concentration.

At the bottom of the steep flow, I haul myself out to the left of the streamlet, and again collapse in exhaustion. My window of light is almost gone, but I cannot care. I sleep immediately, the sleep of total depletion. Waking some time later, shivering and wet, I find that the sunlight has left me. It is not yet dark, but my ravine is again in shadow.

Now before me stretches a steep area of rock that parallels the stream. It curves down to a place where there is a little grassy plateau, about ten feet long and five across. Next to the plateau, my stream collects into a pool, big enough for me to submerge myself, dammed in by large rocks and tangles of brush, decorated by a cluster of small trees that joins the plateau to the pool.

After two nights on hard sloping rock, the bit of grass and the little pool look like nirvana to me. Another twenty yards away, I still determine to try and make it there to camp for the night. My route is across the steep curving rock, littered with small sticks and fist-sized boulders torn from the cliffs above. Choosing now to parallel the stream rather than scootch along in the flow of its water, I begin to ease myself across the rock. Rapidly I discover that intense pain kicks in when I allow my body to tilt. Since the rock slopes down in two directions, descending toward the grassy plateau and also toward the stream, I cannot possibly keep my body level.

Hauling my pack to me, I dig for my cherished mummy bag, carefully chosen for its ultralight covering and fluffy down feathers, and usually protected accordingly. Now, I pull out my precious silver "Vision," wad it into a ball and cram it under my wounded left hip. As I inch my way sideways down the steep slope, it serves as a wedge to keep my body semi-flat. I scootch a few inches down the treacherous slope of the ravine, yank it out, raking it over the sharp rock, and stuff it again under my body, caring only that I can reduce the pain enough to go on. Survival has become paramount to all other considerations.

Today is August the seventh. I am due back in two more days. Pretty soon after that, I figure, my friends and family will start to wonder why I have not come home. They may call the park service and report me missing. My route is on file. If my story reaches headline news, and probably it will, some of the hikers I have passed will remember me. As a lone woman, I am fairly memorable. They will be able to report where I had been on what day. Helicopters will be sent to search for me. There is no way that they could know my exact whereabouts, and no way that I would be seen at the bottom of the shadowed ravine. I should be prepared to signal when the helicopters come.

Thinking ahead to the possible need for a signal fire, I begin gathering up brush and small sticks that I find along the way. There are none much bigger around than my fingers, but I bundle them up, scoot a few inches, then grab them and move them along ahead of me. I figure I will not be able to gather firewood except what I can reach, and I had better collect it while I can. I have plenty of matches left, and also a lighter. I speculate about the dangers of starting a fire that might spread to surrounding brush. I would be unable to escape such a blaze. I think of a burst of flames escaping the boundaries of my small fire and sweeping through the ravine, burning everything in its path, including me. I make a mental note to have extra water handy and to clear some ground around my little pile of brush. I can afford no mistakes.

Finally I reach a rocky little area next to the grassy plateau. Not nearly as flat nor as soft and cushy as it had looked from twenty yards away, the unwelcoming spot nonetheless represents luxury to me in my debilitated state. With a sigh, I lean myself back on the eighteen-inch ledge of dirt that marks the edge of the little plateau. There is no question of getting myself up onto the plateau tonight, so I settle for propping myself against the bank.

Unable to reach my water source, now pooling up a few feet in front and down to my left, I tie a piece of nylon rope securely to my Nalgene bottle. I cast the bottle out into the pool and pull it in. I feel like I'm fishing for water. Sometimes I catch an almost full bottle, sometimes just a few ounces. It is enough. I drink, then prepare to sleep.

I lean gratefully against the supporting embankment. I am filthy, but the moist dirt and crushed grass smells fresh as I sink back against it. I drag my ground cloth and two plastic garbage bags under me, yanking and scootching until I have some semblance of protection from the damp seepage of the moist ground. I pull on my fleece hat, cover my recumbent body and bare legs with my abused sleeping bag, and fall into a restless sleep. It is the comfiest spot I have slept in for the past three nights, almost opulent, I think, as I doze off. Another day has gone by. Today, I've come about fifty yards.

15

The Lure of the Solo Experience

Several months after the fall, I am working my way through the grocery store, holding onto my cart for support.

"Are you the Healdsburg hiker?" asks a woman who overtakes me in the frozen foods aisle. She is middle aged and slightly overweight, with a round pleasant face under a cap of permed hair. I smile at her, having grown accustomed to being recognized.

She asks questions and listens, fascinated, to my story.

"You won't be doing that again, will you?" she suggests in conclusion.

She is referring to my habit of taking to the wilderness by myself. How can I tell her how much this avocation means to me? I long to share with her the joy of my experience. Of course I am planning on doing it again. I work every day toward that goal, yearning for the delights that only a solo journey can bring.

I know that it is not advised to hike alone. But for me, the rewards are far greater than the risks. To live is to risk; and to risk in the pursuit of one's dreams is a chance well taken. Even if I had paid the ultimate price, and died there in the ravine, I would still consider my time in the wilderness to have been well spent.

Many of my peak experiences in this lifetime have been on just such solo adventures. I have cried tears of joy for the beauty of my surroundings, felt myself to be an integral part of the earth and the universe, talked with unseen beings, been touched by the kiss of God.

How can I, in all integrity, claim that this realm of experience is only an ill-advised mistake? Even after all that has happened, I cannot do so.

My mind wanders through the turmoil that sometimes threatens to engulf my everyday world. Often, my life is defined by pain and confusion and duty. In the wilderness, I reach out for emotion, and my awareness touches the glory that surrounds me. I allow joy to replace the disappointments and stresses of my life.

The land itself is my friend. Nature speaks to me in a way that humankind cannot. As I walk, the simplicity of the trailside ways comforts me. The crisp clarity of the mountain air heals me; the high sweet light glistening on white slabs granite lends me its radiance and restores to me the light of my own essence. My spirit exults, bringing my body and soul into perfect focus. My heart expands. I am like my sleeping bag, stuffed too long in a sack, and let out at last. Up above timberline, single pine trees quiver in the relentless brightness, tall and strong, as I feel myself to be. The wilderness touches the pure high note that sings forth the harmony of my own spirit.

Decisions are easy, and life is blessedly simple. I revel in the clear mountain air, the vast silences, the bird song and the wind in the trees, the freedom to simply be who I am. One foot in front of the other. To look forward or to look back. To stop to admire the delicate petal of a flower. To look up and marvel at a magnificent peak. To stay where I am or to move on. My choice in the moment is the choice that guides me.

There are no other voices to interrupt the ecstatic union of self with nature. I feel myself to have a personal relationship with the natural world, and I love the intimacy of being alone in the wild.

I have hiked by myself for years. Occasionally, I pass another solo hiker on the trail. Usually they are men. Once in a long while I pass another woman. I can count them on one hand.

"Aren't you afraid?" people sometimes ask me. I am not. I know that there are dangers. But I am experienced in wilderness travel, and I believe myself to be safe from the crimes common to urban density. It is hard to imagine someone drawn to the life of the criminal bothering to hike hundreds of miles with a heavy pack to perpetrate a crime. Backpackers usually don't carry heavy firearms. I consider myself a fairly unattractive proposition for rape, as sweaty and smelly as I usually am. I do not waste my experience being fearful.

Numerous spiritual traditions honor solitude as a way to become closer to oneself, one's path, and one's relationship with spirit. Some Native Americans speak of the vision quest, New Age seekers go on retreat, and others desire solitude as a way to clear their mind and grow closer to spirit.

I love feeling myself to be one of the wild things. I like to be free from the chatter of other humans, exempt from the awareness of their presence. It touches me that the animals of the forest, afraid of groups of noisy humans, consider me to be one of them, and will come close.

I recall a day when I am sitting on a log eating my dinner out of my cooking pot. A nervous doe, quivering with wildness, snuffles near the edges of my camp. I watch her, making no move to go closer. She watches me. Eventually she settles just a few yards away, sitting passively in the grass, making her dinner out of succulent green shoots. She recognizes a being of like kind and sees that I pose no threat. We finish our meals in quiet companionship.

On another special morning, I open my eyes to find myself eyeball to eyeball with a baby bunny. His wide innocent gaze meets the delighted wonder in my own eyes. As I slowly sit up in my sleeping bag, I see that there are baby bunnies all around, hopping about like popcorn in the grass.

I drop into different spaces of awareness when I spend these treasured days alone. I become at once less self-conscious and more conscious of myself. I have only myself to please. I no longer judge myself as I appear to others. I do not see my reflection in their eyes. I do not wonder what they think of me, whether they find me acceptable, how I smell to them, how we might relate. I become an eccentric. I revel in the pungency of my own body scents. I scratch in inappropriate places, talk to myself, sleep when tired and eat with my fingers when I'm hungry. The longer I am out, the more the layers of social custom are stripped away. I feel released from the pressures of human convention.

In the wilderness, there are no demands except for those of my own desire. Compromise is unknown. The appeals of propriety, of motherhood, of jobs and friendship and the expectation of other people simply do not exist. Whatever I want to do is what I do.

I am rarely lonely during days of solo hiking. I feel less alone than I do amidst the trappings and companionship of civilized society. In urban life, the rules are complex, the communications often obscure. The punishment for not understanding is the cruel slap of isolation amidst the masses.

Sometimes I hike or backpack with friends. Those trips have offered their own rewards, the gifts of companionship and shared experience. The pleasures of social interaction take the place of the joys of solitude. Group hikes also offer the reassurance of safety.

Yet, a group of people no longer has the freedom that I can claim when soloing. There are always elements of concession, the negotiation of people needing to agree, the chatter of other human voices, the pad of many footsteps, the sight of people blocking the clear view of forest and meadow. With a group, it becomes necessary to get reservations in advance, to plan ahead for where to camp, for menus and gear choices and trail selection. A group needs to stay in larger, more trampled campsites. Spontaneity is diminished. The moment-to-moment choice is no longer available, nor is the blessed silence that says so much to my hungry ears. I crave the special gifts that only a solo trek can offer.

Sometimes, driving my car through the world of human creation, oppressed by the constant noise, the pervasive concrete, the continual busy shuffle, the static of uncontained and unsatisfied human energies, I wonder how people could live in such a way without shutting themselves down to an intolerable degree. I feel it like shrapnel in my soul, the constant barrage of ugliness and chaos. How could anyone not desire respite from this world?

Each time I return to the wilderness, I know that I have come home.

16

The Third Day

The third night I dream that I am found. "Hi there," says my friend Edward M. He has heard me calling, and has come to find me. Edward is an easy going, cheerful soul. I am somewhat bewildered by his presence, here in this remote ravine, until he explains that he, his wife, Carmen, and their young daughter, Lorca, are car-camping at the family campground just a quarter of a mile away. I feel a little foolish with my notion that I am alone in the wilderness, but I still need help, and gratefully accept his assurance that they will go back to the drive-in campground and summon assistance. I am saved! Relief washes over me.

So real is the dream, that I look around as I awake, expecting to see my friends. They are not there. Seldom have I felt so disappointed, and never have I felt so alone as I do at this moment. To have dreamed a happy ending so vividly, only to find it snatched away by the cold light of another desolate dawn seems the cruelest of tricks. Bitterness nibbles away at my determination.

A small streamlet, activated during the night, oozes from behind my back, and flows under my resting place, moistening me and all of my gear with a continual steady trickle. A colony of small black ants marches across my prostrate body. Other bugs, busy with purpose, join the activity. I watch them listlessly, powerless to redirect their scurrying, and too weak to care. They pay me no heed. I am too limp to present any impediment to their purpose, and in my loneliness I welcome their company. I recall my first day on the trail, and the hikers who had turned back because of an abundance of insect life.

My whole body aches. I have just two Tylenol tablets left. I had eight with me when I fell, and had been portioning them out, two at a time. I would save the last two for tonight. I doubt they help much anyway.

Again, I go through my morning routine. As I sip at my little cup of instant coffee, still some consolation on this grim morning, I notice that my fuel is running low. Though unable to eat much, hot beverages are a great comfort. I might need my stash of wood to boil water. I stretch out my arms, leaning as far as I can to collect up more little sticks. I study my map once more. I try to eat some dried fruit. I wait for the sun to come into the ravine.

I can delay no longer. My way is blocked by the pool of water, effectively dammed up by a tangle of largish rocks and sticks. I cannot see past the barrier of rocks and trees that creates the little pool. The stream disappears downhill where my eyes cannot follow it. I do not know what lies beyond. To the left of the pool is a small grove of trees, and next to me, to the left of the trees, is the grassy little plateau. I cannot see much past these impediments, but it is clear that only possible path for me is across that plateau. Somehow I must hoist my helpless body up the eighteen-inch rise onto the flat. Until I can do that, I can go no further.

The eighteen-inch height is more daunting than a 4,000 foot climb had been in previous weeks. I cannot pull myself forward, as I cannot turn on my stomach. Having to support all of my weight with my arms alone, I cannot push myself sideways. Pain keeps me from rolling or tilting. With my back to the step, I try pushing up with my arms. My body is a dead weight. I can hardly budge it; I cannot lift it even a few inches off the ground. I try building a ramp with rocks, scrabbled from the surrounding ground. It crushes down as fast as I pile it up. I try stuffing my little stash of firewood under me. It is not enough. I think of jamming my pack under me, but cannot get my body high enough to cram the pack under it. All that long day, I try to maneuver my limp body onto that little plateau. Try as I might, I cannot hoist myself up onto the grassy ledge. My strength is fading. I am running out of ideas.

I am utterly exhausted. Unable to retrace my scooting path uphill along the ravine, and defeated in my plan to continue down the stream and reach the trail, I realize that I will have to stay where I am for another night.

I busy myself making my spot more livable. I carve out a resting place against the bank with my fingers, pushing the dirt around and pulling out rocks and sticks that dig into my body. I save the rocks in case of approaching bears. I pile the sticks carefully to one side for my future signal fire. I have fashioned a sort of chaise lounge out of the dirt, with a reclining backrest for myself, mounds of rocks and earth piled up under my wounded legs, positioning them so as to be as comfortable as possible. I stuff my small piece of blue foam mattress under me, creating a better buffer between the cold moisture of the ground and my body.

Fortunately, I've been constipated since the fall. I have no idea what I will do if I suddenly need to void my bowels. Late that day, I feel pressure in my lower intestines. I rip my shorts up one side with my hiking knife, thinking to push my clothing aside if I have to poop, then somehow drag myself away afterward. It is an unformed plan. I shy away from the thought of sitting there in the muck by my own feces. Have I really sunk this low? I don't have the luxury of considering the options. There simply is no other way. With a sigh of relief, I feel the urge subside. I don't have to deal with the problem after all. I drag together the ragged edges of what were once my favorite hiking shorts and attach them loosely with three safety pins.

The water of the stream, collected in a small pool just below the place where I lie, looks appealing. I would love to haul myself to the pool, filthy as I am, and submerge myself in the fresh clear water. I can almost feel it swirling around me, washing me free of the grime and stench of these last few days. I know the cold water would soothe my injuries. But I am terrified that I will not be able to pull myself back out, so I stay where I am. I take care to drink often. I have no hunger or thirst, but I cannot risk dehydration on top of my other injuries.

Thwarted in my journey, I have time now for other sorts of awareness. I hear the echoes of the water, sparkling droplets making twinkling sounds that echo across the walls of the ravine. The treetops whisper to me like the sound of angel wings.

I talk to myself, to God, to anyone or anything that might be listening. I talk to myself, half demented by now from my increasing desperation and loss of hope. Perhaps I am starting to grow delirious. I put my hand anxiously to my forehead. Is there fever? I can't tell. Will this then be my final resting place?

I fancy that I hear voices. Is it the water, or are they spirit voices calling out to each other? Or to me? I talk aloud to them, to myself. Am I growing closer to the spirit world? I hear what sound like Native American chants in the twinkling sounds that bounce off of the walls of the ravine. I see Brazilian healers. I hear the voices of people that I know. Are they calling out? Are they searching?

I see angelic hosts gathered to celebrate. They are there for me, I know. On one side, there are those who have passed on. I pick out faces, my mom, my dad, my first husband, gone for over twenty years. I see others that have been special to me, and many who I don't remember, hundreds of souls assembled in an etheric army, their numbers stretching out in ranks behind them, on into infinity, assembled, quietly, gravely waiting.

On the other side I see the souls of those who are still alive, my friends and family and loved ones. They too are a silent presence, biding their time patiently to see what will come to pass. Their ranks as well stretch out behind them as far as my eyes can see. So many souls, so many people, touched by my small life, touched by my presence.

I feel in all of them a sense of sacred celebration. There is no pressure, no pleading, no attachment, no fear or sadness. They are here in solemn ceremony, to commemorate this moment. I feel a vast peaceful acceptance from the multitude, and also from within myself. I walk now that narrow path between the living and the dead. Whichever way I turn, my passing shall be consecrated. I feel honored to be thus acknowledged. I feel myself to be one of these spirit beings, a part of this ghostly host.

As I grow accustomed to the spirits I see around me, drawing closer by the hour, I also grow used to life in my ravine. Mine. That's how I think of it. I own this place now. My presence makes it mine, mine by the intensity of my experience, by the depth of my suffering, by the extent of my belief, by the quality of my insights. My ravine. Mine.

The local insect life is growing used to having me here. Various crawling things make temporary homes in my clothing and my gear. The little black ants have by now made my legs a part of their trail as they come and go about their business. The ants don't bite, so I let them continue their busy crawling. I can't stop them anyway.

Oozing water also makes me a part of its path. It seeps in a steady trickle from the bank where I rest, drizzling its way determinedly toward the stream in front of me. It moistens the area underneath me, and permeates the plastic bags that were my vain attempt to keep my body dry.

Weary of my own adventure, I submerge myself instead in my book, letting the brutal lives of the Aztecs provide soothing respite from my own tenuous existence. I have no idea what to do next.

17

Two Toots of a Whistle

Doubting that anyone is out there, but craving the sound of human words, even my own, I have called out randomly, sporadically, during the past few days. Now my voice is one of despair. I don't believe that anyone will hear me. I haven't given up, but I can no longer imagine my own salvation.

"Help! Help me! I'm tired of this!"

I'm ready to be rescued now!

"Help!… Help me!… I'm tired of this!….HEEEELP…I'm ready to be rescued!" I call out from time to time, wailing my despair into the empty wilderness and using my voice to alleviate the constant pain. A scream of agony becomes instead a cry for help.

"Heeeeeelp me!"

And then I hear it. So faint that at first I think it some trick of the winds that are my only companions, whispering their wordless voices through the ravine. I hear it. Two tiny toots of a whistle.

That is all I hear. Two tiny toots, so faint that they might be a dream. Pausing for a moment, I call "HELP! HELP ME!" again, this time straining my lungs for top volume. I stop to listen anxiously for an answer. It comes again, the two gentle toots. Had I imagined the small sounds, were they the whispers of the canyon spirits, growing seemingly closer by the day? Or perhaps it is a group of hikers in a festive mood, simply tooting for fun.

I become manic in my need. I know that this is my only chance. I become frantic; the fear that hope will be snatched away erases the calm that served me so well during the previous days and nights. I open my mouth and scream, a pure high sound issued forth at the maximal volume that my tired lungs can produce.

The previous year I had invested an inordinate sum in a lovely featherweight titanium pot with a lid. I love my little pot. Now I grab it and bang desperately on the bottom with the lid, denting it badly in my efforts. I hear the two toots again. And a voice. Or was it a voice? I cannot tell what direction it is coming from. I cannot hear what it said. I try banging on my pot, two answering bangs. There is silence. To my despairing ears, it seems to last an eternity. Long moments go by. They are gone, they have left. They don't believe me. They didn't really hear me, can't find me. They don't want to be bothered.

Again, I hear sounds. They seem no closer, but now they sound like voices. I cannot hear the voices clearly, and I do not know if they have heard me. I cannot jump up, I can not scramble through the brush in the direction of the sounds. I feel the restrictions of my immobility keenly. All I can do is yell. And hope.

I scream again, at the top of my lungs, this time a raw, harsh sound that has no room in it for words. I go for top volume as I put all of my terror and dismay and longing into that shriek. I bang harder on the pot and shout even more wildly.

"HEEEELP! I need help! Don't leave me!"

Despair sets in as the voices and the whistle cease. Then again I hear them, now a little closer. This time they seem to be a bit below me, out of sight down the ravine. I shout out my circumstances.

"Help me! I need HELP! I HAVE BROKEN LEGS! HELP!"

This time I hear a responding voice, I'm sure of it. I cannot hear what it says, over the now deafening echoes of the gurgling stream against the ravine walls. It sounds like a man's voice. What if he gives up, if they give up. What if they can't find me.

I grab my water carrier, actually the bottom half of a gallon milk jug, out of my pack, and feverishly whack a hole in the bottom. The container isn't shaped much like a megaphone; it has a flat bottom, and doesn't taper out at the sides, but I will grasp at any hope. I plunge my jackknife into the bottom, and saw out a squarish hole, perhaps two inches across. Putting the makeshift amplifier to my mouth, I call out again.

I hear the voices, and then they cease. I am alone again. There is only silence from the wilderness.

18

Contact

The stench of despair is heavy upon me. Bitterness drags at my spirit. They are gone. I am ready to admit defeat. I sit there by the embankment, shorts soaked in mud and urine, bugs crawling over me, tank top stained with rings of sweat and splotches of water. My shorts are ripped up one side, held together by safety pins. I smell dreadful. My face is blackened with bruising, body smeared with dirt and covered with scratches, puffy feet still encased in soggy, sour hiking socks, right knee swaddled in a bundle of sodden rags, both legs now swollen hideously.

Then I hear a noise. Someone is there. They have not left. Somebody is scrambling down the hillside across the ravine from where I sit. I burrow in my pack for my comb and toothbrush. If I am going to be rescued, I want to look good.

The hillside is very steep, a treacherous scramble with an overlay of loose dirt and leaves providing little foot purchase. A peppering of scrubby poison oak offers unfortunate handholds. The fear from my own sudden plunge still fresh within my memory, I worry lest my rescuer slip as well. Bits of rock and dirt tumble to the ravine floor, as I fight down visions of falling, directing my attention elsewhere and trying not to watch.

Some minutes later, I peek through the trees and catch my first glimpse of the person who has climbed down the slope, now standing on firm ground. I cannot begin to say what that first sight of humanity meant to me, after the solitary desperation of those long days and nights. I had thought that I would never see another human being. Now, I am no longer alone. Overwhelmed by the totality of my relief, I burst into tears. It is the first time that I have cried since the fall.

I supposed later that Jake was a good looking man. He was tall, maybe six foot, of about my age, with shortish dark hair, thick but turning to gray a little at the edges. He was built like a hiker, lean but fit, dressed in hiking clothes and wearing a daypack.

I don't notice any of this at the time. It doesn't matter what he looks like or who he is. He is surely an angel in human form, sent to find me. Somehow, in hundreds of thousands of acres of empty wilderness, he has heard me, has felt the desperation of my situation and the intensity of my need. He is the miracle that I have been hoping for.

Jake climbs carefully over the rocky ground toward me, pausing to honor the moment with a Buddhist gassho, placing his palms together, and bowing briefly over them, a nod of reverence to the moment, to my salvation, to his own part in this most miraculous circumstance. We both feel the sanctity of the occasion.

"I'm not going to leave you." Somehow he knows just what to say. I cry still harder, smiling through my tears. I am not alone any more.

"I'm Jake," he says.

"I'm Amy."

"Can I put my arm around you?" asks Jake, sensing that human touch is what I need most at this moment, but not knowing how badly injured I might be. All he knows is that something horrible has happened. I nod my consent, and he puts his arm around me, gently and without hesitation. Stinky, smelly, wounded, incredibly blessed me.

19

The Three Rescuers

I think of them as my three Buddhist angels, Jake, Leslie and Walter. They don't seem comfortable with the concept. Perhaps Buddhists don't have angels. But here they are, the three of them, suddenly, miraculously here.

There is perfection in the number three. I think of the trinity, of the strength of a three-sided triangle, of the many threes that are ritualized in mythology and honored in scientific knowledge.

These three travelers are the perfect three people to effect my rescue. They are sturdy hikers, all of them, just two days into an eleven-day loop through Kings Canyon National Park. They started out at the Rancheria trailhead near Wishon Reservoir, in the Western Sierra, about eighteen miles from where they find me, and have planned a ninety-mile backpack loop through the Tehipite, next going east up the Middle Fork Kings River, to intersect with the John Muir Trail going north. At Muir Pass, they planned to take a cross-country route through the Ionian Basin that would connect up with the trail over Hell for Sure Pass, and eventually finish their trip at Courtright Reservoir.

Jake Van Akkeren and Leslie Bartholic are husband and wife, fifty-four and fifty. They had met sixteen years ago on a Sierra Club hike that Jake was leading on Mount Diablo. Before that, they had both enjoyed solo backpack experiences, so they are not judgmental about my choice. They can understand what I am doing out here by myself. Both are teachers, practical and pragmatic, calm in the face of unexpected calamity.

They are with their friend Walter Keiser, fifty-six, a member of the same Buddhist temple that they attend, the Berkeley Zen Center. Walter is a highly motivated and very successful urban planner. He

Three wilderness angels, Walter, Leslie and Jake (left to right).

is also a long distance runner, as dedicated to his job as he is a fanatic about his pursuit of outdoor recreation. An expert in wilderness medicine, he himself had broken two ribs and torn a rotator cuff in his shoulder a few weeks previously while helping to implement a rescue during a whitewater rafting trip.

The trio had almost cancelled their planned trip because of Walter's injuries, but had decided to go anyway. These are most likely the only three people who have hiked into the Tehipite in the past three days. I know what my fate would have been if they had decided to cancel. A chill goes up my spine. I feel the touch of divine purpose, and understand that these three have been sent to find me, guided by some force greater than any of us. It is not just chance that they are here now to pluck me out of this vast expanse of deserted wilderness. I don't believe in coincidence. I do believe in miracles.

At the time when Jake hears me, he and Leslie are working their way down the trail into the Tehipite, the same trail that I had lost some three days previously. A fast hiker, Walter has gone on ahead, and is already down in the valley below. He thought he heard a call, but figured it was someone temporarily lost from a group.

"Do you hear something?" Jake asks Leslie, as they pause on the trail near where I lie. He thinks at first that it might be a wounded animal.

"No," she says, "But let's listen."

And so they do.

Jake has had some hearing loss. I don't know how hard of hearing he is, exactly. He makes light of it. I do know that he has trouble picking up certain frequencies. But Jake somehow hears my call, and somehow intuits that this is no random shout. He subconsciously senses that a life is in danger and perceives the intensity of my need. Whatever the specific nature of his awareness, there is no doubt in my mind that his perception saved my life.

After some calling and whistling, listening for responses, Leslie and Jake decide that yes, I am a real person, and yes, I do need help. After more exploration, whistling, and calling to me, they establish my approximate location. Because of my position in the echoing ravine, I cannot hear what they say, but they can hear my words as they come closer to where I am trapped. Jake leaves Leslie on the trail with most of their gear, equips his daypack with basic necessities, including a first aid kit, and sets out to climb down to where I am stranded.

Jake finds me in the ravine. After establishing that I have enough food, water, and warmth, he plans to go back and discuss with Leslie and Walter how best to organize my rescue. He promises to return shortly, to camp near me where I am stranded so that I will not be left alone. I trust in Jake, so I assent.

Jake climbs back up to the path, on the slope high above me, where Leslie is waiting. They mark the spot to be sure of finding it again. Leslie goes on down the trail about a mile and a quarter to the Tehipite Valley to tell Walter what has happened, and send him back to consult with Jake. Reluctant to leave me for long, Jake climbs back down to my spot, and sets up camp a few feet away, on the little plateau that had been my goal for the past two days.

I am looking bad, face dark blue with bruising, like a black eye over the entire surface, broken tooth gouging into my lip and nose swollen. My arms are covered with huge bruises as well. Both legs, especially the right, are by now grotesquely bloated. I have grown somewhat accustomed to the sight, but to Jake they are a shock. I give him as many details about my injuries as I can supply. He does what he can with his first aid kit, washing the open scrapes and cuts, and applying fresh antibiotic lotion and clean bandages. We both know that it is not enough. It is imperative that we get me out of the ravine as soon as possible.

The flush of my sudden salvation starting to fade, I worry a bit about how repellent I must be to Jake. I smell terrible even to myself, and I am embarrassed that I can still only pee sitting there in my clothes. "I don't mind," Jake tells me when I express my dismay. "I really don't." He explains that he has spent years caring for an invalid mother. He reassures me in such a clear, no-nonsense way, that I believe him, and quit fussing.

He applies himself to using my purifier to pump water for both of us, mixing up electrolyte replacement drinks, and trying to get me to eat. He has brought with him tempting goodies like veggie jerky and homemade dried pears. I want to please Jake, but I cannot choke much down.

Eventually Walter scrambles down the slope to join Jake and me, and make plans for my continued care and eventual extraction. Walter is tall and wiry, with a lean, worried look that I later identify as focused concentration. He takes my temperature, and my pulse, and checks the pupils of my eyes, but makes no comment. I accept half a Vicodin pill from a small supply that he carries for the pain of his own injuries.

He and Jake sit near me, and refine the rescue plan. I listen, but contribute little except an occasional nod of agreement. I am sorry to be spoiling their vacation, and feel pathetically grateful that they are willing to go to such lengths to help me. But I feel safe. Content to put myself in their hands, I am starting to lose strength.

My three angels are exhausted as well, having tackled the punishing descent into the Tehipite earlier that same day. It is by now late evening, nighttime threatening to close in. We will all sleep that night, Jake near me since I clearly can't be moved, and Leslie and Walter in the valley below. Tomorrow morning, Walter will run back up that formidable trail, 4,000 feet of elevation gain in just three miles, to get to the rim, then six more miles to Crown Valley, nine miles in all. We have all hiked past Crown Valley. There are several small cabins, probably one of the few private holdings that remain within the park. We concur that we've seen people there. We do not know if there will still be anyone around, or if they can be of any assistance, but the camp represents the closest possibility of finding help. If nobody is there, Walter will have to continue on, running the entire nineteen miles to the Wishon trailhead.

Out of my earshot, Walter and Jake consult about my condition and possible fate. Walter has considerable knowledge concerning wilderness first aid, and he gives Jake his diagnosis. It doesn't look good. I have an elevated temperature, a fast shallow heartbeat, and dilated pupils. These are all signs that infection is catching up with me. Knowing that the onset of septic shock from bacterial invasion is swift, and probably deadly in these circumstances, Walter warns Jake.

"She might not make it." Jake wisely conceals this thought from me. I am blithely unconcerned, certain now that I have been saved, and having total faith in my three rescuers to do whatever is needed to ensure my deliverance.

Walter gives Jake specific instructions about how best to treat my injuries. The powwow complete, Walter scrambles back up the slope, leaving me in Jake's care. The plan has been made.

20

The Fourth Day

Dawn comes early to my ravine. I awake in my now accustomed spot by the embankment, aching in every limb, but mercifully unaware of my continuing peril.

Jake, a short distance away on the grassy plateau, has no such illusions. He knows I could still die, and I am his responsibility. Unbeknownst to me, Jake has lain awake all night long, listening to the erratic sound of my breathing and the twinkling gurgle of water echoing sweetly against the walls of our ravine. Bursts of meteor showers illuminated the night sky as he kept the long vigil. Could he keep me alive by watching over me? What would he do if I took a sudden turn for the worse? Fortunately, we never have to find out. We have made it safely to another sunrise.

This morning, Walter will climb up that dauntingly steep unmaintained trail out of the Tehipite, nine brutal miles of relentless uphill, the equivalent of running out of the Grand Canyon. If nobody is at Crown Valley, he will have to run another ten miles before he reaches the trailhead and the car, and can go for help. I think about how tired he must be, after hiking nine miles the previous day, then climbing back up to where I am stranded, and down again to the valley. I know that Walter is still recovering from two broken ribs. Will he be able to make it? My rescue now depends on him. Then I remember his frown of concentration, the tension in his shoulders, the driven quality that speaks of unyielding determination. I understand that sort of resolve, and feel reassured. Whatever it takes, Walter will make it.

Walter will blow his whistle to signal us as he goes by on the trail up above, out of sight of where we rest. Two toots mean "Is everything OK?" Our two answering whistles will reassure him: "Yes. Everything is fine." If we respond with three toots, we are in trouble. What Jake doesn't tell me is that two toots mean that I am still alive, three mean no. The rescue crew will want to know what to expect. Are they saving a live person, or taking out a corpse? Jake asks me to listen for the whistle; he is not confident that he will be able to discern it. Mid-morning we hear the signal and respond with two toots. Walter is on his way.

Leslie is camped in the valley below, a calm presence, ready to signal the helicopters, serve as liaison to rescue crews, or do whatever else is necessary.

Jake tells me his plan for our day. First he will cook me breakfast. Then he will purify enough water for both of us, and mix up several bottles of sports beverage to replace any lack in vital fluid balance. He will put a solar shower full of water in the sunshine, so that I might have a wash and feel refreshed. We will while away the hours reading, snacking (he is determined to get me to eat) and getting to know one another. It is a good plan. I am soothed. The calm practicality of his plan provides reassurance in our extraordinary circumstances.

The pain in my leg and hip is constant but not intolerable, especially since I am not now trying to drag myself across the rocks. Perhaps I am just growing accustomed to it, a continual throb in my experience. I keep myself as comfortable as I can, moving as little as possible. Jake has charge of a small vial of vicodin pills, leftover from Walter's bout with broken ribs. I am reluctant to take any, as I resist taking drugs of any sort, but I do finally take one. And a half. They don't seem to have much effect.

I am eager for more help to arrive. We both are. I calculate in my head that late afternoon is the earliest we might hear any signs of rescue. If Walter does not find help at Crown Valley, it might be much longer. I know he is a long distance runner, but still, the trail is rugged. It will take him a while. I counsel myself to patience. I have a lot of patience these days. Impatience is one of the luxuries that disappeared along with my mobility.

I am fearfully weak, but I feel about as OK as I can under the circumstances. I am still lucid and cheerful, though I have huge bruises over most of my body, and my legs and feet are now grotesquely disfigured, swollen to a hideous dark red, skin stretched tight over inflamed flesh.

Jake spends the day taking care of me. Using the contents of Walter's first aid kit, he redresses my wounds and applies fresh bandages. There is not much more that he can do for my injuries. Every couple of hours, he plies me with beverages. As promised, he feeds us both. I worry about depleting the food supplies of my new friends. I know that they, like me, have carried everything in the packs on their backs. My rescuer assures me that they have plenty. I can hardly swallow; food does not look at all appetizing, but I cannot bear to disappoint Jake, so I choke down a few mouthfuls. He heats warm water in his solar shower and pours it over me, still in my filthy shorts and tank top. What a wonderful sensation! Still sitting in the dirt and still having to pee in my clothes, I nevertheless relish the illusion of cleanliness. When the sun grows high, Jake uses my tarp to erect a shelter to shield us from the wicked midday heat. We compare routes, look at maps, read a little, and discuss trails and trail food, the things that hikers talk about.

Like a baby animal opening its eyes and assigning motherhood to the first living thing it sets eyes upon, I adore Jake. I am grateful to all three of my rescuers, but he is the first human being I had seen for five days, the first human I never thought to see again. I think of him as my wilderness angel.

"You are my mountain sister," he tells me. It is a bond like no other.

Jake and I chat about where we've hiked and compare our favorite parts of Sequoia/Kings Canyon. We both love the wild places, and that is a comfort. Despite our desperate situation, we cherish the sights, sounds and smells of this beautiful spot. A small waterfall plunges downward and twinkles in the light farther up the creek; leaves whisper in the wind as they cast dappled shadows over moist mosses and sculpted rocks. Our ravine is exquisitely beautiful.

After hearing my story, Jake is curious about the scene of my fall. He makes a foray back upstream, locating the site by the splotch of blood on the rock where I had fallen. Neither one of us wants to be responsible for leaving debris to disfigure the landscape, so he retrieves my boots, and also collects up the bits of silk that have ripped off my shirt, still snagged on the bushes along my path.

He tells me he did not find my hiking pole. I picture it still stuck in a tree sixty feet up that fierce slope. I cringe inwardly, fear for him and remembrance of my own fall combining into one terror; I make him promise not to try and retrieve it. I imagine my trekking pole, decades from now, found by some chance hiker. The rubber parts will have decayed by then. All that will be left will be the pieces of titanium-aluminum alloy that make up the shaft. Will someone find them and wonder? Will anyone guess at my tale?

After exploring the ravine, Jake shares his belief that he would not have heard me if I had stayed where I had fallen. I am stunned by the implications. By what inspiration had I been drawn to attempt that gritty journey down the ravine? Surely it was part of the miracle that I had managed to drag myself to where I could be heard.

"You wouldn't have made it any farther," Jake tells me. There is an impassable drop-off, a cliff, just past the spot where I have made my last stand. I would not have made it down the ravine into the Tehipite.

WALTER'S STORY

At about 9 A.M. that same morning, August eighth, Walter bids Leslie goodbye, and sets out up the trail from the valley, ignoring a lingering ache from his still-taped ribs and injured shoulder. He passes the sign, an arrow on a piece of paper, that marks my location in the ravine. Two toots of his whistle receive two answering toots from Jake and me. "Good," he thinks. "She is still alive." He pushes to the limit of his endurance, forcing himself up the steep grade, and running much of the way. How far will he have to go? He doesn't know. Two and a half to three hours later, feeling his strength failing, he struggles at last toward Crown Valley, where he hears sounds of children laughing, and sees that there are people at the encampment. Hopefully, he approaches the small cluster of summer cabins.

He blurts out his story. This is indeed a private camp, owned by a group of firefighters from Reedley, California, an agriculturally based city of about 21,000. They are here now on a fishing holiday with their kids. Fire Chief Mark Johnson is among them. Trained for quick reaction in the face of disaster, Mark saddles up the fastest horse even as Walter continues with his story, writing a note telling of my condition and giving directions to my exact location.

No sooner has the information been relayed, than Mark is off and riding hard toward the trailhead that provides the nearest cell phone access, some ten mountainous miles away. From there, he retrieves his cell phone from his car and calls 911. The California Highway Patrol (CHP) helicopter, already in the air, is the first to hear the call and respond. An hour later, a park service helicopter is also deployed, and on its way to the Tehipite.

Walter didn't know what to expect as he ran toward that fishing camp. He didn't know if anyone would be there, or if they would feel inclined to help. He desperately needed assistance, for if he found none, he knew that he couldn't have made it to the trailhead before late afternoon. There wouldn't have been time to locate me before dusk, and it would then have taken another entire day for me to be rescued. As he suspected, that extra day would have cost me my life.

The firefighters from Reedley, though trained for rescue in their daily jobs, had no obligation to help Walter other than that of human kindness. They were just people on holiday with their children, motivated by integrity and inspired by crisis to do what they could for strangers in need. The willingness of those firefighters to respond to Walter's story made the difference between life and death for me.

Now exhausted, Walter is vastly relieved to have passed the rescue operation into other capable hands. He has done his part, and done it well. His heroic run up out of the Tehipite will not have been in vain. Mark will make it to the trailhead within a couple of hours, and with Walter's clear directions, finding me should be easy for the rescue teams. I can be carried out that same day.

The firefighters are kind, professional and supportive to this unknown person who emerges suddenly from the woods. They make Walter welcome as he takes a much-needed break, having a shower and playing for a while with the children. As a Buddhist, Walter generally doesn't eat meat or drink alcohol, but in this situation, he gratefully accepts a beef burrito and a cold beer. Not long after one, inspired by this new evidence of the goodness of humanity, and restored by food and rest, he heads back down the trail to verify that I have been found, and that the rescue is progressing well. Reaching the rim of the canyon once more, he hears helicopter sounds. Good. The rescue is in progress.

Rescue

In the beautiful Tehipite Valley below, Walter has set Leslie to laying out a huge cross, the international symbol of distress. The cross is on the ground, about twenty feet by twenty feet, and is constructed with double rows of stones, sure to be seen easily from the air. This is meant to serve as a marker for the helicopters, and as a landing site.

Late in the afternoon, Jake and I, in our ravine, finally hear signs of rescue. Jake, continuing with his plan, is preparing to cook me soup for dinner. He does not hear the sounds at first. The echoes are confusing, bouncing off the rock walls. But when I identify the first hum of a helicopter, we are both excited. We hurry to get organized for our exodus from the ravine. We spread out any brightly colored items we can find. Jake runs about flapping my purple ground cloth, intending to signal our location.

I am certain that rescue is only minutes away. My companion, however, is sure that the helicopter passing overhead has not seen us. The sounds retreat, and Jake once again wisely keeps his dismay and his fears for me to himself.

Another helicopter, with a slightly different sound, enters our vicinity. Again, it passes overhead, but appears not to see us. I am blithely unaware, thinking only that the sounds mean I will shortly be carried to safety. Jake grows more concerned. How will they find us in this dark cleft? From overhead, we must be virtually invisible, despite our efforts to be seen.

Realizing the necessity for some high visibility signal, he considers building a fire, just as I had done in the days before he had arrived. Jake reflects on the possibility of winds whipped up by the helicopters igniting the wilderness into wildfire, burning up thousands of acres of forest, and us along with it. He does not share these thoughts with me either—not until many months later.

Now that I believe I am safe, I worry about my gear. It has become even more precious to me, having sustained me during the long days and nights of my ordeal. I have a sentimental attachment to my abused down bag, my trusty GoLite pack, even my dented little pot. Still unwilling or unable to accede that I may not walk again, much less backpack in these mountains, I consider that I will need my gear for future trips. I wonder how we can manage to salvage my equipment. How will it be recovered? I am still certain that rescue is imminent.

As Jake had guessed, the first helicopter, the large CHP medical rescue copter, had been unable to find us, and had been daunted by the unexpected necessity of landing in a deep narrow valley like the Tehipite. It had come and gone. The next helicopter was from the park service, and the pilot was accustomed to maneuvering through the dangerous terrain of the Sierra wilderness reaches. But he too was unable to find us. Despite Walter's directions, Jake and I are virtually invisible in the narrow ravine.

Jake and I continue to listen intently. After what seems like a long time, we finally hear more sounds. A helicopter hovers overhead, circles a bit, and this time Jake is certain that it has seen us. He is right.

In the ravine we still wait. Finally, on the same slope that had brought me Jake, we hear the scrambling that announces that more assistance is here. As I peer through the leafy trees, trying to make out who has come to save me, I see that help has arrived in the form of a young woman in a park ranger's uniform, climbing nimbly down the treacherous slope. Strong independent female that I am, in my hour of need I have somehow reverted to a more neolithic picture of my own rescue. I had imagined six burly young men with a stretcher who would come and carry me off to safety, unerringly supported on their strong shoulders.

"It's a woman," says Jake in my ear, confirming my slight doubt at the appearance of my rescuer. Debbie Brenchly appears to stand about five-foot-two and weigh around a hundred pounds. She has little gear, and she is alone. But when she goes to work, my concerns are immediately put to rest.

Without delay, she gets on her radio and begins rattling off statistics about my location and probable condition. She talks while she works, taking my vital signs, rapidly extracting every bit of pertinent information about me, my fall and my circumstances, as she unwraps my bandages. A highly skilled wilderness medic, she explains everything to me as she goes along.

Following shortly behind Debbie comes Fred Mason, whose arrival she has announced in advance, introducing him with a smile as "my New England sherpa." Fred is as described: a large, hearty young man, the epitome of cheer and robust good health, also a highly skilled emergency medical technician. He has a rosy smiling face, and carries Debbie's heavy pack as well as his own, with no more bother than if they were a couple of daypacks. The two of them make an impressive team, rapidly assessing my injuries while bantering back and forth all the while.

"We are your rangers until we get you out of here," they assure me. They are prepared to camp with me in the ravine until I can be extracted. They have been brought by the park service helicopter, and have hiked up from the valley below, where Walter, now back in the Tehipite, had explained my exact location.

Debbie unwraps my mangled right knee. I take a quick peek, but can hardly bear to look at it. The sight is startling. A gaping hole marks the place where a knee had once been, and the torn flesh has adopted the bright reds and blues and greens of the silk sarong I had used as a bandage. "It's not as bad as it looks," I assure my rangers, although none of us are at all sure this is true. I describe the transient qualities of the Indian dyes used in my makeshift bandage.

Alternately talking on the radio and caring for me, Debbie has by now quickly and efficiently inserted an IV into my arm. She radios in to the park service helicopter, now parked in the Tehipite Valley, for permission to inject two milligrams of morphine, and hooks me up to a bag of fluids.

Jake is vastly relieved when Debbie Brenchly arrives. Gratefully, he has passed me into the capable hands of these two rangers, but he still lingers nearby. He is assigned to hold the IV bag while Debbie takes a photo, for documentation and as a souvenir.

I won't see the photo until much later. There I am, sitting in the ravine with Jake next to me, holding the bag of IV fluids. Behind us are the treacherous rocky streambed onto which I had fallen and the long steep route of my determined scootch. My legs are swollen hid-

Amy and Jake in the ravine.

eously. My face is black as a bruise. A dark hole shows where a front tooth used to be. I'm wearing a fresh white bandage on my knee and grinning from ear to ear.

"We've rescued a lot of people," says Debbie. She turns out to be the foremost rescue ranger in the National Park Service. "But rarely anyone as badly injured as Amy, and never anyone as happy." Of course I am happy. I am going to live. I had not expected it to be so.

Dangling by a Thread

Two helicopters are now safely parked in the Tehipite. Neither can land in the ravine, and neither can carry enough fuel to hover for long over our location. They also cannot fly after dark. The park service copter brought the team of rescue rangers. The police helicopter is needed for its lift capabilities, which the smaller park service vehicle does not have.

Two plans for getting me out are being considered. The first plan entails strapping me into a stretcher, using climbing gear to winch me up the slope to the trail, and having a team carry me the mile and a quarter to the valley below, where the police helicopter will be waiting to rush me to the hospital. This would have to happen the following day, by which time a climbing team could be summoned to the remote place where I am stranded. To my delirious mind, this proposal sounds simple and painless. In reality, being hauled up and jolted out over the steep rocky trail would have been a nightmare.

The second plan is more alarming to me. It involves being airlifted out of the ravine by the police helicopter. I would dangle far below the helicopter, strapped into a litter and swinging by two long straps.

But plan B is the favored choice. My rescuers share a growing concern over my condition. I remain giddy with relief at my miraculous reprieve and oblivious to their apprehension, though my condition is grim. I've now been in the ravine for four days and nights with several severe fractures, one of them open and almost certainly badly infected.

This second plan is favored because I need significant medical care as soon as possible.

Evening is closing in. Declining light threatens the rescue attempt. We are running out of time.

"I'm not going to lie to you," Debbie tells me. "It's going to hurt like hell." I nod my consent and my understanding. She and Fred have been rapidly assessing the possibilities for rescue while calling down to the valley on their two-way radio.

The plan is explained to me. The police helicopter will fly over the ravine, guided there by a red smoke flare set off by Debbie and Fred. The copter will lower down a litter, a metal stretcher-like contraption, which it will leave with us. The rangers will have just a few minutes to strap me in securely. The helicopter cannot continue hovering, but it will return and lift me in my litter, high above the Tehipite, by two small straps, one attached to the head, one to the foot. Debbie and Fred will control the wild swing of the litter from down below with two ropes.

"Don't worry," they tell me. "We took a seminar on this just last weekend." I am utterly terrified.

The roaring of the helicopter announces its arrival. It hovers high overhead, lowering the stretcher toward us. The air from the whirling blades shoots through the narrow ravine, kicking up tornado-like winds, sending debris, water, and pine needles flying about us. The sound is intense, magnified in the narrow space and bouncing off the rock walls. The rangers wear protective goggles and earplugs. Jake and I shield our faces with our arms, as Debbie and Fred race to grab two dangling ropes and guide the descending litter to our location.

Quickly, the rangers and Jake hoist me into the litter. It is tricked out with something that looks ominously like a canvas body bag. I am efficiently strapped in, legs held flat, arms crossed over my chest. "Don't open your eyes," warns Debbie. I have no intention of doing so.

At the moment in which I find myself strapped into the stretcher, I can at last let go of the need to hold on. With the letting go of responsibility, the full volume of the pain kicks in. Despite the morphine, I am almost senseless with agony.

There is more noise, more running, more scurrying around me. The helicopter, for some reason, cannot hoist me from our present position. Fred, Debbie, and Jake must carry me up the ravine to a more open place. Eyes squinched tightly shut, I feel the jerky motion as they lift me up and stagger with me back along the streambed, up the treacherous ravine. I hear Jake breathing unevenly, and feel each jolt, as my rescuers struggle with my dead weight. Two days it took me to traverse that slope, and they do it in a few minutes. I feel their anxiety, but I am too lost in my own pain and fear to be concerned for them. Each bump brings excruciating pain, as the stretcher tilts my injured left hip against its metal bar with each step.

The sun has begun to sink, and already we are cast into shadow. We have only a few more minutes to complete my rescue.

Amidst more shouts, and another wind that threatens to flatten us to the floor of the ravine, I am hooked up by long straps to the helicopter, soon to be airborne. The last time I was in midair, I crashed to the ground. Mustn't think about that now. Eyes still tightly shut, I pray only that it will be over soon. I am terrified of heights, and can easily imagine falling helplessly through the air from high above. "If you were going to die, you would have already," supplies my wishful mind. And with that dim reassurance, I am launched into midair.

"How long will it take?" I had asked Debbie, knowing that I can endure anything for a finite amount of time. "Three minutes," she replied. Now I rely on a device that has gotten me through many an intolerable situation. I count. I focus my mind on the reassurance of the numbers. One thousand and one, I count, arms crossed over my chest, eyes scrunched tight shut. One thousand and two. One thousand and three, and so on up to one thousand one hundred. When I find that my trial is not over yet, I begin again. One thousand and one. I focus my attention on the numbers; they have a beginning and an end. Each comes after the one before, in an orderly, expected way. One thousand and two. I must keep track. Four times I count to one hundred, and then it is over. My helicopter has landed me in the Tehipite Valley.

Opening my eyes, I find that the helicopter is on the ground, and I am next to it. I have a dim impression of several people rushing about. Walter and Leslie are there. I summon some civility through my haze of terrified pain. I thank Walter, then say hello to Leslie, whom I have not yet met. I have a quick impression of a small person with a smiling face.

"I've heard a lot about you," I say, remembering what Jake has told me about their life together, and wanting to acknowledge her part in my rescue as well. "You're a good cook," I add, recalling the dried pears.

Completing my transformation from tough and self-reliant to thoroughly helpless, I squeal in pain as one foot is accidentally bumped against the doorway of the helicopter.

"Good," thinks Walter. "She's human." He is relieved that I am able to feel pain, knowing it to be a sign that I have not gone too far into shock. It is also good that I have made the shift toward beginning to comprehend the psychological implications of all that has happened. I am loaded, still in my litter, into the CHP Medical Helicopter. Then I am off on the ride to the University Medical Center in Fresno.

I had said goodbye to Jake in the ravine just before I was strapped into the stretcher. I sensed his concern. I knew that he felt responsible for me, having saved my life. He was worried too that I would lose my leg. Understanding my love for the wilderness, he surely knew

The helicopter.

what that would mean to me. But he didn't mention amputation, and I did not consider the possibility. Perhaps my mind just blocked out the worst, or maybe it was my freshly reinforced belief in miracles that reassured me. Despite the rising levels of pain, I was convinced that everything would somehow be alright.

"Do you have everything?" Jake had coached me before I was lifted away. "Your ID? Your health insurance card?"

"Yes," I say. I don't want to lie to Jake, but I am too embarrassed to tell him that I don't have health insurance.

I am terrified that as soon as the hospital realizes that I cannot pay, I will be refused medical assistance. Through the excruciating pain, I pray that nobody will find out until I have been patched up and put back together.

23

Repairing Amy

wo solemn, chisel-jawed medics staff the CHP helicopter that carries me from the Tehipite to the safety of the hospital. One navigates the short flight to Fresno while the second works at inserting a new IV into my arm. The one that Debbie had installed in the field has wrenched itself out.

Realizing that my life is more endangered with each passing minute, these two men disregard their own peril in their determination to see me safe. It is already dusk when my helicopter lifts off from the valley floor. Flying within deep narrow canyons is a challenge in the best of times, dimming light and treacherous down-canyon winds adding to the risk. The men in the helicopter do not waver. I am carried to safety, and to them, as well, I owe my life.

My damaged legs are still strapped flat in the metal stretcher. I had kept them slightly bent the entire time in the ravine, but now they are restrained in the most painful position of all, no doubt to keep me from further damage. I've already been dragging myself around for days, bones dangling, but the med techs don't realize the irony of my current immobilization.

I am beside myself with pain, hardly able to think, it so consumes me. All the pain that was muted during the long lonely days and nights has come back full force. Debbie's two milligrams of morphine have hardly touched it. I try my childbirth breathing, but can only sob and groan through each breath. I try counting, using the same device that got me through the terrifying lift out of the ravine. Can I make it to a hundred? Yes. And again. The straps have been loosened slightly at my pleading, and morphine from the newly installed IV is finally starting to kick in. After what seems an eternity, in actuality only twelve minutes after we take off from the Tehipite Valley, we reach the rooftop of the University Medical Center in Fresno.

I am rushed out of the helicopter and downstairs to the emergency room (ER). Still conscious, I am so involved now in my own pain that I notice little else. I have a vague impression of people swarming around me like locusts, many of them, asking me questions and rapidly but carefully stripping off my clothing. I've already sawed my shorts up one side, and I relinquish them to the hospital staff. But I insist on saving my favorite tank top, struggling to sit up and pulling it off myself. Now that I am going to live, I might be needing it again. I answer questions coherently, though I remember little of it later and cannot recognize my own signature on the forms that were pushed at me. I refuse to allow anyone to flex my legs. The pain is too great. But for the most part, I passively accept whatever is done to me.

After that come dim impressions of arsenals of metallic equipment, vague disturbing dreams, and rides through narrow corridors on a wheeled gurney. I gaze up at anonymous faces. How did I get here? I can't remember. I doze in and out. At some point, my doctor introduces himself. I have an indistinct vision of bright-eyed interest and concern, but cannot remember his name.

Despite my confusion, I am thoughtlessly, wordlessly joyful through it all. I have been saved! I am going to live. I have no doubts at all, now that I am in the capable hands of the UMC personnel. I grin like a fool through proddings and pokings and needle pricks and rubber tubes.

"She is a smiling happy woman laying on the gurney," says the hospital report. I give no instructions. I make no plans. I have no requests. I relinquish myself entirely into their care. And I am happy to do so.

The University Medical Center in Fresno is a Level I Trauma Center. It is also a world class teaching hospital, affiliated with the University of California, San Francisco, Fresno Medical Education Program. Both of these aspects are fortunate for someone like me. Level I offers the highest level in emergency care, and the medical professionals here are some of the best in their fields. If I had been injured in some other place, I might have fallen into the hands of a small-town doctor who sees a case like mine once in ten years, but instead, I have a team of surgeons who are at the top of their game, and who repair mangled flesh on a daily basis.

Two handsome young interns stop by my gurney to tell me how honored they are to be assisting in my surgery. I gaze up in confusion at their earnest faces, and nod graciously. I doze off again. I wake up to find that I'm being wheeled along a hallway. I'm not sure what day it is, or what time.

"You have to call someone," they tell me. My girlfriend Carla's number is the only one I can remember. OK then, I'll call Carla. What an adventure she'll think it! I lie on my gurney while they dial and hand the phone across the desk.

Carla is a statuesque five-foot-eleven with an abundant shock of curly red hair; one of the warmest, most loving, and also one of the busiest people I know. She is the single mom of a teenage son, works full time, and has a growing private healing practice. She maintains an impressive number of close personal relationships. Because of the continual overwhelm of an incredibly hectic life, Carla rarely picks up her phone at all. She never considers picking up for an early morning call.

Unbeknownst to me, it is now 6:00 A.M., the morning after I had been flown in. Somehow Carla knows to answer her phone. "Guess where I am!" I chortle.

I would realize much later that I was heading into major surgery, and that the hospital staff wanted me to call someone, preferably a next-of-kin, in case I died. It sometimes happens. At the time, I think only of sharing my great adventure story with my friend. I don't remember much of the conversation. They wheel me away.

When next I become aware, I am looking up at Carla's beloved face, surrounded by a halo of gold. An angel with Carla's face, I think through my haze. It is Carla's blonde-haired sister Diane, who lives in Fresno, summoned at a few hours' notice to be with me so I will not be alone when I awake from surgery. Two hundred and fifty miles from home, I welcome the sight of a smiling and familiar face. Diane has a job and two children of her own. I have met Diane only once, some years ago at a Thanksgiving feast, but she has dropped everything to come and be with me. The first of many tears of helpless gratitude trickle out of my eyes.

I awaken after those initial surgeries with a foot-long incision stapled together down my left thigh. My entire right leg, stretched out on the bed in front of me, is heavily swathed in white bandages. The ankle is in a plaster cast. A formidable bundle of gauze and a detachable knee brace immobilize my knee. A tube drains the knee wound. I have an IV in my arm and a urinary catheter, attached to a drainage bag. I cannot roll at all to either side, or lift my body enough to squeeze a bedpan under it.

I hear the diagnosis. I have two fractures of the left hip. It was not simply dislocated, as I had thought. Both major and minor trochanters are broken clean through. I now have a metal bracket in my hip. That wound was clean. The patella, the kneecap, in my right knee is shattered. The open knee fracture is more problematic, badly infected after

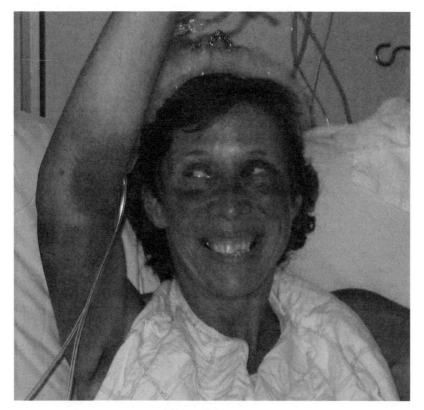

Amy in the hospital.

four days, untreated, in less than sterile conditions. What was left of my patella has been wired together, and a metal plate set in place behind it. My right ankle is dislocated, and I have hairline fractures of the right tibia (in my foot) and the left femur. When I arrived, I was about two quarts low on blood, and despite Jake's efforts, fairly dehydrated. Ongoing infection is the greatest concern.

Later they tell me that in just one more day the right leg might have been lost, and the infections would have become systemic, impacting my vital organs. My arrival at the hospital could have been too late to save my leg, or my life. I am very lucky to have been found, and luckier still to have been rescued when I was. Just one more day and it would have been too late.

All of this flows over me. I am heavily drugged, these long days in the hospital, morphine suppressing the worst of the pain. Impressions are confusing. I am sometimes grateful, often despairing, and occasionally lucid, only to forget later what I have said and done.

I am much more badly injured than I had known. My mind cannot attach just yet to how very bad it is. I narrow the focus of my glazed psyche, using the same device I had used in the ravine, looking ahead only to what I can handle, fastening upon the next meal, or the next pain medication. I can surely make it through the next hour, the next few minutes. I cannot think farther than that without desperation. I feel more helpless than I ever did in the ravine.

I know, because the medical staff marvels, that I am incredibly lucky to be alive. I am also extraordinarily fortunate not to have sustained even more serious harm. I have no back or spinal damage, no concussion, no fractured pelvis, no internal injuries or even any broken ribs. My nose and my entire face are severely bruised, but they will heal. My front tooth can be replaced. My arms and hands are entirely intact. I have none of the complications that should have come with an accident like mine. My injuries, though critical, are nowhere near as bad as expected after a sixty-foot fall.

Awash with emotion of many kinds, I feel raw and vulnerable like never before. Tears ooze out at the slightest provocation. Any sort of sentiment seems close to the surface. I cry with gratitude, with joy, and also with despondency and remembered terror, as the true horror of my experience begins to seep back into my consciousness. I weep with fear for my own future. The tears mingle together, an almost constant gush of raw, swirling emotion, as I lay passive in my hospital bed. Overwhelmed by it all, I am still amazed to be, against all odds, alive.

It seems that everyone here has heard my story. Even in a place where traumatic injury is commonplace, I am special. I find that I am considered something of a hero. This bewilders me. I don't attribute much courage to myself. I just figure I did what I had to do. Surely anyone would have done the same in a similar circumstance. Giving up was, after all, not an option. People come to gape, to congratulate me, to interview me, to shake my hand.

I find, from chatting with the continually changing staff, that I am a prime piece of flesh.

"Your case is unusual," says one orderly. "Everyone wants a piece of you." UMC is in a rough neighborhood, with a service area of 15,000 square miles, home to a large indigent population. I am a welcome change from the gunshot and knife victims, drug overdose casualties and declining diabetics that seem to comprise many of the other patients. I had been fit and healthy before the injury, but I am also badly injured, with a multitude of problems. I am a medical challenge, but one with a high likelihood of success. This also means that I am constantly surrounded by doctors and students. I don't care. I have long since given up any claim to privacy.

Once cherishing the freedom and space of being alone in the wilderness, I am trapped now in a small room with three other women. I am evidently the worst injured among us. The others can all stand up, with some help, and I cannot even turn onto my side. The next bed is scarcely three feet away. There is so little space between the beds that two people cannot walk around them at once. A thin curtain separates me from my neighbor. Her toilet commode is only two feet away from my bed. When she gets up to use it, I can see the curtain billow with her form, and hear the sound of her defecation.

The hospital bill tells me later that my room is "semi-private," but it seems more like a train station. Two television sets compete constantly with their noise. Swarms of visitors come and go, one or two at a time, or whole families, talking and laughing and eating and staring curiously at me as they go by.

The hospital staff scurries in and out. There are nurses, doctors, anesthesiologists, nutritionists, interns, aides, and a host of others I cannot classify, including gaggles of students and assorted teachers, all poking, prodding and asking me questions. It takes me some time to identify the multitude, and their various jobs. I am never alone.

The infection in my right knee is proving very difficult to suppress, so every day or two I am readied again, and taken to surgery. Nothing can be done about the gaping hole in my leg until the infection is controlled. Six more times, I am prepped and anesthetized for surgery. Six times, the complicated figure eight wires that hold together my shattered kneecap are removed, the wound debrided, cleansed of any trace of infection, and new wires installed. The steel plate behind the four broken pieces of patella is removed and replaced as well. The wound is left open and bandaged up again. My body reels from the effect of infection, shock, and ongoing surgeries.

I grow grimly accustomed to the pre-op routine. No food or water after eigtht at night, on through the morning. In the late morning, they come to get me for surgery, wheeling me away down the hall, still trapped in my hospital bed, to the operating room where I am anesthetized for another round of scraping and new wiring of my shattered knee. I awake again in late afternoon, confused and ill from the cornucopia of anesthetic drugs, aching with pain from fresh surgery.

Days pass in a fog. Antibiotics drip continually into my arm. Shots of morphine and other painkillers come on a regular basis. Too weak to do otherwise, I accept the frequent invasions of my body, lying passive as needles thrust, tubes tighten, doctors and x-ray techs poke and push and mutter over my limp form.

I like Dr. Appleton, my primary surgeon. He is an assistant chief of surgery, an osteopath, just come here from New York City. I have a quick impression of youth, enthusiasm and energy. His hair stands a bit on end, and in his eyes is the gleam of the fanatic. I know that look. Here is a perfectionist who will stop at nothing to do the finest job possible. I know the gleam of light that identifies people who believe intensely in their work. He has that gleam. Even through my despair, I am reassured.

A few days after I have arrived, someone gets around to asking me if I have health insurance. I have been dreading this moment. I had paid for health care coverage privately for over two decades, but I let it slide a couple of years ago, when costs rose dramatically. Being phenomenally healthy, I had not made a single claim in twenty years. Now I need health care badly, and I am uninsured.

Will they eject me as suddenly as I was admitted? Will I be wheeled out onto the street in my hospital bed, left to somehow make my own way home, still unable to walk, crawl, stand, or even sit in a wheelchair? I have heard rumors of medical assistance denied to those unfortunates who have no health insurance, of people left on the street to die, of emergency care refused.

None of these things happen, though between surgeries, I do begin to get calls from accounting asking how I intend to pay. My bill is already up to $165,000. I have no idea how I will pay the hospital. Someone brings me a Medi-Cal application. Too ill and confused to understand the process, I am incapable of using my once-sharp mind to unravel the possibilities and financial ramifications. I lay there in a drugged blur and sign anything they give me. I am at their mercy.

Gone is the strong independent woman, advocate for herself and participant in her destiny. I cannot pay for my care. I cannot leave. So weak am I, and so painful are my injuries, that I cannot even sit up without assistance. Nurses worry that I will get bedsores from being so long in one position, I who once exulted in covering miles with my long legs, in seeking new vistas every day.

My world, once defined by glorious expanses of blue sky and mountain peaks, has been narrowed to this small room. I can see no grass, no trees. I cannot even open the window to get a whiff of fresh air. I lie here in a haze of pain, too ill to even long for what I miss so much.

Day after day, I lie quietly, entirely dependent on these strange people whose assistance I need so badly and into whose control I have fallen. I am grateful for the help, but I want desperately to depart from this place. People come and go, bustling around me, wheeling me in my bed in and out, defining the hours of my days with a seemingly endless multiplicity of drugs, tests, procedures, and questions. Nobody seems willing or able to tell me what final prognosis I may hope for, or when I might be able to leave.

24

An Unknown Wilderness

The hospital is unknown territory to me, a wilderness in my experience. I understand the Sierra, and feel at home there. Even isolated in the backcountry with serious injuries, I had felt it to be a friendly place. This new situation is much less comprehensible. Confused, overwhelmed, and helpless as I am, this feels to me to be a dangerous environment, threatening by its very strangeness. For the sake of my own welfare and survival, I set out to learn the ways of this unfamiliar wilderness.

UMC is a rough place. There are armed guards in many of the hallways. A visiting friend reports a rumor that the ER is closed periodically to thwart the drug raids that seem commonplace. I wonder if she is right. Occasionally an alarm will go off. I ask what it is and am told it is a fire alarm that automatically blocks off sections of the hospital. I consider what would happen to me if the place should catch on fire. One of the nurses, reading my expression, swears she will carry me out in her arms if need be.

My floor is, "the floor where they try to lose the least amount of money," explains an RN delicately. One man lies in bed and hollers, "Help me!" continually, all day long. His calls echo through the hallway. Of the three other women in my room, only one speaks any English. She uses her command of the language to hurl abuse at anyone who comes to help her. We share a buzzer, which she leans on constantly. The staff, used to her demands, often ignores it.

This is evidently an old hospital, and not an affluent one. The building itself is decrepit. A new facility is being built, but it is not finished yet. I learn that some things are in short supply. There is no hot water in half of the building. The hot water heater is so old that the parts cannot be found, someone tells me. The ice machine is several floors down. If I ask for ice, someone has to run down on the elevator to fetch it. The hospital beds are new, but are a bit too big for aged doorways. My bed bangs against doorframes, jolting my broken body each time I am wheeled in or out.

"Hold onto your pillow," one aide tells me, as I'm headed again for surgery. "If you lose it, you may not get another." A patient down the hall is busy ripping his pillow up in a fit of temper.

The hospital is not allowed to supply fans, though the air conditioning is ineffectual against the one hundred five-degree heat outside. Fear of liability, I am told. A kindly nurse takes pity on my limp sweaty self, and finds me a fan that another patient has left behind.

They also cannot supply talcum powder, although it would cut down significantly on the discomfort of sweating continually on stiff rubber-backed hospital sheets. It's another liability issue, they say. Any white powder might be anthrax.

Worst of all, there is a toilet paper shortage. After using the few sheets that I have been allotted, I ask for a roll. That is impossible, I am told. I have diarrhea from the constant stream of antibiotics, and I need toilet paper. I spend the better part of a day trying to track down a roll. I get only blank looks. I cannot go raid one of the hall bathrooms myself, as I would have done if my legs were functioning. How am I supposed to wipe my hands and my butt after I use my bedpan? And how is it that I am expected to eat with those same filthy hands? I cannot get up to wash them. It seems absurd to me that despite the scrupulous care of my injuries, such basic rules of hygiene are overlooked.

Finally, I ask the cleaning lady, a sweet soul who quietly and efficiently does the dirty work, always with a smile and a nod for me. She gives me a roll of precious toilet paper from her cart. I am so delighted that the next day she gives me two, instructing me to hide it away. Ah luxury! Rolls of toilet paper make me ecstatic with joy. I protect my little stash carefully.

The surgical staff seems excellent, but always in a hurry. The support staff is compassionate and skilled, but vastly overworked. Experience tells me that it takes anywhere from two minutes to an hour and a half for my bedside buzzer to be answered. I plan carefully for my comfort and survival. I try not to be a bother, and learn to have what I need within arm's reach, in case I cannot get anyone to help me. I arrange my snacks, water pitcher, reading material, and phone, all within easy distance. I train myself to wedge my own bedpan under my limp body, though often it takes a while for someone to come and take it away after I have used it. Sometimes I have a dirty bedpan and a food tray all balanced on my bed at the same time.

I find that during the hour and a half of shift change, which happens twice daily, there is usually nobody to respond to any request. The nurses are busy transferring information and having meetings, and I may not be able to get help. I find out when the shifts change, and make sure to stock up on water and dry towels and whatever else I may need before it happens. I memorize the name of my new head nurse at the beginning of each shift. Sometimes I have the same one, but usually not. I have about fourteen nurses in my stay in the hospital.

I learn that I will get pain medication if I ask, but if I ask too often, I am looked upon with suspicion. There are too many addicts here in the hospital. I inquire as to my medication schedule, and then ask only when more meds are due, though the pain is still very bad. I find out the intervals allotted between pain medications, and make sure that they never wear off during shift change.

Essential care in this strange place is good. My vital signs are taken often; my IVs replaced whenever needed, my pain levels monitored well.

Inessentials are less forthcoming. I find I can usually get fresh sheets or a new hospital gown if I ask. I stockpile clean linens if someone comes by with a cart. I learn to accumulate towels to mop myself up after the night sweats in case no dry sheets are available. Every few days I can get a bed-bath, or help to wash my hair. I might be able to get someone to help me prop myself sideways to prevent bedsores, but maybe not. I try to stuff pillows under myself. I am instructed by my doctors to keep my right leg elevated, and I attempt to do that for myself as well, with extra pillows purchased for me by my friends. The staff often does not have time to help, and I am only allotted one pillow from the hospital.

I had nothing when I arrived at UMC except the clothes I was wearing—now cut off me and discarded, or stuffed in a very smelly plastic sack—and a Ziplock bag with a few dollars, an ID and a credit card. I have friends bring me the things that are lacking: extra pillows, bottled water, skin lotions, a comb and brush, pens and notebooks, books and magazines, a pocket fan and a few reassuring odds and ends from home.

My friends raid local thrift shops for clothing that I can wear when I am better, or tug on over my bandages. They supply a briefcase for the paperwork, and a wheeled walker for when I can walk again, if I can. A huge bottle of talcum powder adorns my bedside table, and a box of baby wipes so I can clean my hands. They bring me teddy bears, a nail file, reading material, chocolates, cookies, instant noodles, any sort of food that might tempt my resistant taste buds. They supply vitamins and natural healing supplements.

I set about making the angry woman in the next bed my friend, and making myself agreeable to the hospital staff. It seems prudent to be polite, and it is not difficult. They are all helping me, and I am extremely grateful for their care. I hear later that they call me "the nice lady." I don't think of myself as a lady, not do I feel particularly amiable. Why wouldn't I be kind to the people who are helping to save my life?

After a week or two, I develop a nasty intestinal infection. It's endemic to hospitals, the nurses tell me: a secondary disease brought about by all the antibiotics. I am highly contagious, oozing with rank-smelling, bright yellow diarrhea. I am quarantined in a private room. I am alone at last, freed from the constant stream of other people's visitors and blaring TVs eating into what little peace I had behind my thin curtain. I smell terrible but luxuriate in the blessed silence. Ironically, the cure is a six-week course of Flagyl antibiotic, the same drug used to kill giardia, the parasite that sometimes pollutes backcountry water sources.

Seeing the quarantine sign, the cafeteria staff occasionally leaves my tray outside my door. Sometimes nobody remembers to bring it in to me. I don't particularly care. I can hardly eat and become scrawnier by the day. Already thin from my ravine ordeal, my flesh now hangs loosely from my bones, sagging, prune-like, with no muscle and flesh to support the skin. Finally I'm as skinny as I always wanted to be, and it's not what I thought at all. Not a svelte vision of health and slender fitness, I am instead a weak, exhausted, emaciated invalid.

The food that arrives on a metal tray three times a day is so repellent as to make me nauseous. For the first time in my life, food looks to me like the enemy. It disgusts me to see it and smell it. The hospital food is horrible, huge globs of unidentified meat substances slathered in slimy gravy, reconstituted mashed potatoes, overcooked vegetables and pallid canned fruit, although we are in the California Central Valley where much of the best produce is freshly grown. I swear to myself that I will not protest, but complaints sneak out anyhow.

One nurse explains that many of the patients love the food here. I keep my doubt to myself, and let her continue. A lot of them are homeless people, she tells me, and this is as good as they ever have it. Three hot meals a day, and a clean bed. I am overwhelmed by the implications of what she says. I want desperately to get out of this place, and this is the very best that some people can hope for.

She tells me a story about a little boy with a leg injury who was in the hospital last year. His whole family came to visit him three times a day. The tray of food that was brought to the little boy's bedside was all the food that the family had to eat. They shared his meals with him. I cry for that little boy and his family. I have never had to go hungry a day in my life. But I still cannot eat the food.

Later, when I am finally able to sit up in a wheelchair, I roll myself triumphantly to the elevator, maneuvering in and out with difficulty, intent on my goal. I have tucked a few dollars into my cast and memorized the route to the cafeteria. Perhaps there will be something there that looks edible. I arrive at the cafeteria, and try to buy an egg salad sandwich and an apple. "We can't sell you that," they tell me, eyeing my hospital gown and my plastic ID bracelet. Diabetic patients will sneak down and try to buy food. They can't take the chance that I may be one of them. I go next to the gift shop, where a kind woman helps me reach cookies, candy and chips. I wheel triumphantly back to my room with my supply. I still can't eat much, and I continue to grow skinnier.

Carla's sister, Diane, brings me a steak dinner with all the trimmings one night, and it is the best thing I've had in a month.

On one singular evening, when I'm feeling a little better, I am able to get a hold of a phone book. After negotiating for a doctor's special order, and with much cooperation from the nursing station, I manage to get permission to have a pizza delivered to my quarantine room. With the works. I can only eat two pieces, but it's worth it.

After two weeks in the hospital, the physical therapists begin to come every day for a half hour or an hour. They are clearly very busy, and I drop everything whenever they make one of their unscheduled visits. I know, even at that early date, that they are the people on whom I must depend if I am ever to walk again.

At first, our exercises involve simply being able to scootch into a wheelchair from my bed with the help of a sliding board. It requires two strong therapists and extra painkillers to maneuver me to the chair that first day. My left leg is propped up slightly bent, and the right, still casted, sticks straight out, tied to the leg rest with a sheet so it won't slip off. I am triumphant, but can only sit for ten minutes or so. They encourage me to do isometrics and to work on my arm strength. Am I training for life in a wheelchair? I wonder. Nobody has really said if I will walk again. A week of hard work later, I can get to the chair with minimal assistance and no sliding board. I want more, I tell them. I am released in my chair for half an hour at a time, to prowl around the hospital. I manage to wheel myself outside into the sunshine, and find a tree to sit under.

25

Almira

When first installed at UMC, I share a hospital room with three other women. The bed next to me is occupied by Almira. Being day and night in close proximity, I come to know her well. She whines constantly, cries pathetically, and verbally berates anyone who comes to help her, screaming epithets at the staff and making continual demands. Often her requests seem to be pleas for attention, as she will call for ice, then ask for it again, forgetting that she has already gotten some. Only a few feet away, I am privy to it all.

"I want water! I want my meds! Why can't I get my food? It huuuuurts. It's time for more meds!" She seems primarily to want more pain medication. I wonder to myself if morphine addiction has taken the place of whatever she was on before.

"Nurse! Nurse! NURSE! I want to talk to my nurse! Get me my nurse!" The whining and shouting goes on and on. Her TV plays constantly in the background. She punctuates her calls by leaning on our shared buzzer. Buzzzzzz. Buzzzzzzzzz. Buzzzzzzzzzzzzzzzzzzz.

"It's the only way to get anything," she tells me, offering up a bit of wisdom for my benefit. She has spent long periods of time in the hospital, and seems to be a regular. A few of the hospital staff seem to pity her, but most simply ignore our abused buzzer.

Almira becomes both my nemesis and my teacher. I recognize in her a part of myself, a destructive part that just wants to whine and pout, that says that life isn't fair, it's probably somebody else's fault anyhow, so don't bother trying. It is the part that wants to give up. At the same time, she teaches me gratitude for my own existence. The quality of her life tells me how very blessed I am with my own.

A picture of Almira's life emerges from what I overhear. Though fairly young, perhaps in her early twenties, she has several children. They all get some sort of government assistance, as does Almira, because of some disability that I can't identify. Her family, mother, uncle, boyfriend, and so forth, vie to keep Almira with them so they can have "her money." It can't be much, but evidently financial gain is what defines Almira's worth in their minds. She is often in the hospital, currently because her boyfriend beat her up, injected drugs into her belly, and punched her in the stomach. She insists that he loves her.

She is being treated for a drug overdose and various internal injuries. She can get up, but can only walk a few steps unsupported. She refuses to do anything to help herself, and feigns sleep when the physical therapists come around. I suspect, from hearing snippets about her life, that being in the hospital is the best that the world has to offer Almira. No wonder she is resistant to getting better.

Almira is no fool. She too listens to what goes on around her. She finds that I am getting snappier care and better treatment by being polite to the hospital staff. She alters her own abusive attitude and finds that a different approach gets her better care as well.

Almira speaks English and Spanish with equal ease. She is fluently bilingual, much more so than any of the hospital personnel. In the days of her improved attitude, she takes it upon herself to interpret between the patients and the staff. She is kind, compassionate and helpful, walking about and assisting the other two women in our room. She does an excellent job, and thrives under the praise.

I see her in the hall one day, walking reluctantly with the help of a brawny physical therapist and a walker. I myself still can't even stand up, though I want desperately to do so, and have only just been able to get into a wheelchair.

"Alright, Almira!" I tell her. "I'd sure be walking if I could." It seems to register that there is some way in which she is more fortunate than I. After that, she appears to look forward to walking, and even brags about it to her aunt on the phone. The staff appreciates the changes in Almira.

She can be a sweet girl, though she has clearly had a rough life. She has few visitors. A baby doll that her aunt has given her says prayers when she squeezes it. It seems to be a comfort to Almira. I offer her some ice cream, and introduce her to my visiting friends. She seems touched by these gestures. She asks through the curtain if she can call me "sister" and offers me a stick of gum.

There is talk of sending Almira home. She goes into a decline, regressing to her customary hostility. But she is well enough to be released from the hospital, and off she goes. She will stay with her aunt. The following week I see her again. We are both laying on gurneys, downstairs in x-ray.

"Hi, Almira," I say. "How are you?"

"Not good." She shakes her head hopelessly back and forth. Almira is back.

Is there hope for her? I wish it to be so. Surely there is good in Almira, though it has been tainted by the blows that the world has dealt her. She is smart and helpful. But the cards are stacked against her. Will she be able to break through to a better life? I've seen her on those few days when she did, and I hope that she can somehow make the jump. I am doubtful, but I send a prayer, wishing her well.

One day in the hospital, I've just had another round of surgery. I'm in pain, frankly crabby, and I just want to lay in my bed and feel sorry for myself. Despite my usual resolve, I don't want to go out and practice in the wheelchair. My favorite PT arrives, a hunky young man full of energy and enthusiasm.

"I've become Almira!" I wail. He laughs and goes easy on me this one day. He knows exactly what I mean.

In the rough weeks and months that are to come, I sometimes find it difficult to stay cheerful and hopeful and motivated. I find myself fighting exhaustion and pain, tiring of the uphill battle, wanting just to pull the covers over my head and whine and cry and give up. I think of these times as "Almira moments," and use her story to remind myself not to stay there.

I also use her tale to help me remember how fortunate I am. I think about how similar I am to Almira. Two women with two lives, side by side in two hospital beds, our stories running parallel for those few weeks. Then we once again go our separate ways. I have had advantages in my life that she has not. Who is to say that I would not be like her, had I been less lucky, less determined, or born in a different place, of different parents. I could have been her, I think, and I cannot criticize her for her weakness.

Almira has made my own life a little bit better. I compare my life to hers, and find it good. I see her flaws, and determine not to mimic them. I am grateful for all of this, and I wish her well, sending with the thought a little bit of the good fortune that has been mine.

26

Helping Amy

That one early-morning call from the hospital mobilizes my communities. Carla calls my brother Dan in Washington state, her own sister Diane in Fresno, and posts a quick announcement to a local Sonoma County e-mail list, WaCCO, short for West County Community Online. My friends have been alerted.

I've known Carla since 1994. We met at a tantra workshop and bonded early in our acquaintance, seeing kindred spirits in each other, and sharing the joys and challenges of raising sons alone. Years ago, on a fun holiday to Reno, we swore lifelong support to one another. Our mutual loyalty has survived the trials of the years.

Carla has not forgotten our promise. Leaving a brief message for her boss, Eddie, she takes off to see me for a few days without a backward glance. Breaking all speed limits on the 250-mile drive from Sonoma County to Fresno, she arrives at the hospital the day after I am out of surgery, with her son and mine in tow.

My appearance, thin and gaunt, with a face as black as a mummified corpse, does little to reassure. My independent sixteen-year-old, Sam, is desperately worried for his mom. How is it that I had thought he wouldn't care if I didn't come back? Clearly he cares a great deal. I am very glad to see him, and to see Carla as well. Carla writes to the WaCCO list:

"It was a lot for her son to have to witness, but he, like his mother, has an amazing spirit and inner strength. Amy can rest assured that she has raised a strong and beautiful young man who is anxious to help as much as possible. He was glad he was there, but said he can hardly wait just to have her home again."

Diane provides lodging for Carla and the boys, and entertains the two traumatized teenagers.

Members of the WaCCO list notify others who know me, the availability of the Internet speeding the process. News of my accident spreads like wildfire through my many social circles. The tale of my miraculous rescue becomes headline news, and still more folks find out. Many of the people I know have never met each other, coming from many different social strata and several diverse groups. Now they unite in a common cause. They organize to help me.

Some of my friends are women from my women's circles, with whom I have laughed and wept, shared joys and sadness. Many are single people who have banded together to support one another in a world more friendly to couples. Others are business acquaintances or people I have met only once or twice at events.

They come from communities that feel set apart from the social mainstream by their unconventional relationship choices, or they are ordinary folk who live in my neighborhood. They are people who

Amy with friend, Francesca, in hospital. August, 2003.

know me, who have known me, or have never met me and have simply heard my story and been inspired. They are pagans and Christians and Buddhists and atheists and agnostics. They are gypsies and artists with unusual lives, or intelligent sensitive people who feel too much. They are friends of my parents, parents of my friends, acquaintances and former lovers, and single parents. They are adopted family, or siblings of my own blood.

Very different from each other, from many walks of life, they now share a common goal. Inspired by their pride in me, and united in their desire to help, my need is the focal point that brings together this diverse group of people. I remember my vision in the ravine, the silent masses gathered to celebrate, and recognize this multitude from that vision. They are here now, to acknowledge my survival, my return from that uncertain place between life and death, and to restore to me the life that is still mine. I have never felt so loved. Or so blessed. For the first time ever, I feel truly welcome in my life.

"Have I got something for you!" says a nurse early in my hospital stay. I figure it is more painkillers. I hope so. When I open my eyes, I see not another hypodermic, but an outlandish display of the most rambunctious flowers I have ever seen. An explosion of tropical splendor meets my startled gaze. Five-foot long tendrils reach relentlessly up toward the sky, exotic blooms shamelessly displaying their sensual lushness, petals splayed wide in brilliant hues, stamens proudly erect in the center. I recognize birds of paradise, golden roses with blood red outer petals, and other foliage too rare for me to identify.

"Writer Girlies" says the tag, and I recognize my friend Mary's inimitable touch in the relentlessly sexual joy of the abundant tangle of jungle in my Fresno hospital room.

Now people start coming from floors around to see "The Flowers" and consider me with new regard. Being in a writing group gains me respect, and having the best flowers around gets me more.

"You must know creative people," says one of the nurses.

"You must be special," comments another.

"People must love you a lot," voices a third.

Sally, Francesca, and Adrian arrive at the hospital within a few days. Sally is a longtime friend. Francesca is in my writing group, and

I had dated Adrian for a few months, though it hadn't seemed to be working out particularly well. Now they are all here to do whatever they can to help. I am rarely alone.

Sally camps out in Fresno for a week, sometimes sleeping in her car in the parking lot, fetching things I need, serving as go-between with the nursing station, and visiting for long hours each day. Adrian and Francesca busy themselves managing my business affairs, fielding the correspondence from the many people who want to know what is happening, and running errands to make my hospital stay more bearable. Diane is a frequent visitor. Carla continues to reassure my terrified son, and advocates for me with the hospital staff and the financial aid department. All of my friends visit frequently to give me hugs and reassure themselves that I really will be OK.

We dub all my visitors my "brothers and sisters." Apparently the hospital does not recognize bonds other than birth-blood. But these people are, to me, my family, the people who would and do care for me in time of disaster. Surely they are the brothers and sisters of my heart, if not of my blood.

I am swamped with letters and cards and donations and offers of help; I am engulfed in care and concern. I retreat into my own weakness and let it all flow around me, tears of raw emotion trickling constantly. This new representation of love is harder for me to bear than all of the pain and terror of my ordeal. How can it be that I deserve so much? Yet all of these people believe that I do. The windowsill by my bed overflows with cards and books and flowers, stuffed animals, boxes of chocolates, and baskets of fruit. Sam brings me a huge purple teddy bear.

Now I am known for my dramatic story, my amazing flowers, and also for the quality and quantity of my visitors. The staff sees me differently. I have friends, lots of friends. Interesting, intelligent and colorful ones. People care about me. I am loved.

I see myself differently too. I, who had thought that my life, and my passing, would provide only the slightest of ripples, I, who had felt myself to be so alone that no one would miss me when I was gone, find myself surrounded by people who cherish me. A self-employed single mom, both parents dead for over ten years, living alone, working for myself, now physically incapable and financially destitute, I would have been the last person to expect any help. Yet in my time of greatest need, I find that I am not abandoned, but held close in the arms of the many who love me. I begin to see myself as one of them, alone no longer, an island no more.

Sally calls Jake. He, Leslie, and Walter had originally factored one extra day into their backpacking trip. That was the day that they had used to save my life. They had then continued on with their own journey, not knowing how I would fare. Now they are back from the wilderness. They are delighted to hear that I will live, and that I have both of my legs.

When I am well enough, though still in the hospital, I grow concerned about my primary business and main source of income, Instant Pool Cards™. The business is a one-woman show. I have no employees; I do everything myself.

Determined to provide a solution, Adrian prevails upon me to let him go to my house and collect up what is needed to fill the back orders, continuing to flow in all during the time that I am in the hospital. One afternoon, in between x-rays, blood pressure checks, and IV changes, I talk him through the process via the phone. It takes all of my energy for that day to do this.

Adrian collects up the inventory from my garage, and he takes stacks of pool cards, shipping boxes, brochures, and my database to Carla's house. She, with a workforce of herself, her son, and mine, spends long nights, after completing her own job, filling orders. My brother, Dan, and his wife, Kelly, fly in to help as well. In one heroic weekend, they pack up enough cards to last for three more months. Adrian upgrades my web site, something I have not had time to do. My business is saved. Orders are late, but Sam includes a handwritten note with each one, and most customers understand. They too send notes of congratulation on my miraculous recovery.

Dan and Kelly stay in my house and clean it from top to bottom, anticipating the day when I will be able to move back in. I still cannot care for myself, still cannot imagine being able to go home.

My spirited friends Leela, and Barry, moderator of our WaCCO e-list, are organizing a fund-raiser, with assistance from other WaCCO members. The event will be an elaborate silent auction featuring donations from friends and acquaintances all over several counties.

I cannot help. Lying here, too weak with illness and drugs to ask for the many things I need so badly, I can scarcely even identify what I need. I let it all happen around me. I am inconceivably grateful, yet cannot acknowledge that either. I can do nothing but acquiesce, weeping tears of helpless gratitude, quietly accepting as my friends busily put my life back together for me. I let them figure it all out. And they do.

Amidst the tangle of tubes and cords that surrounds my bed, my friends hook me up with e-mail. As I see two thousand messages downloading, I begin to sob. There is no way I can handle all those messages. They take the laptop away again. Francesca prints out some of the notes from well-wishers to bring to me, and takes care of the massive amounts of electronic correspondence. I am too weak to handle communications, almost too exhausted to pick up the phone.

"There's a web site about you," they tell me. Molly's husband, Miles, has set up a site at http://www.helpingamy.com to accept online donations. Francesca coordinates the content, telling my story with maps and pictures. Sharon, of the Women's School for Healing Arts and Sciences, is looking into tax-deductible status for the donations.

"There's a Yahoo! group for you." Tears flow even more. Francesca has started a Yahoo! group called HelpingAmy, so that people who care about me can be easily informed of my progress.

I am still too frail and ill to do much but take it all in and cry often. I have no words to acknowledge the many gifts, the support, and the love. I, once so strong and independent, have at last learned the lesson of accepting help. I now have no choice but to believe in these diverse people who give so generously of their time and energy. I am more moved than I ever was during my lonely ordeal, terrifying rescue, many surgeries, and the uncertainties of recovery. This tangible evidence that I am loved touches me more deeply than any of that. The world is a better place than I ever knew it to be, and I am honored to be sharing it with people like these.

How is it that I thought my life had meant nothing? How had I believed that nobody would notice if I quietly slipped away? How very wrong I had been, and how grateful I am to be alive for the learning of this lesson.

27

The Purple Ambulance

Finally the day arrives when I am allowed to leave University Medical Center in Fresno. It is August thirtieth, three weeks from the day that I was flown in by helicopter, and rushed to the emergency room. Lou, Coleen, and Adrian have come to extract me from the hospital.

Lou and Coleen are a colorful pair. They favor gaudy bizarre clothing, usually in the color purple, which they often share. They also have hearts of gold. In addition to their own jobs, they both care for Lou's mom, bedridden and requiring round-the-clock attention. Today, they have hired a caretaker for her so that they might come and carry me to safety.

I want desperately to leave this place. I am perishing within these walls. My spirit is dying. I am still losing weight. I show signs of developing secondary diseases of the sort brought on by lengthy hospital stays. I long to be outside, to be in a real home, to see trees and grass and sky, to feel the wind on my face, to be near my friends. This long-awaited day is finally here, and I am ecstatic with joy.

I am also terrified. As much as I want to be away from the hospital, it has become a known quantity in my life. In the hospital, I know what to expect, what sorts of help I may receive. I rely upon the well-trained army of nurses and aides to give me pain medication, help me with my bedpan, sit me up, change my bedding, to do essentially everything for me.

My knee injury has now been opened up and debraded six times, the wound cleansed and wires replaced. Finally, my surgeons are satisfied that most of the infection has been controlled. I had my final surgery just one week ago. A team of surgeons led by Dr. Sian, assistant chief of surgery specializing in plastics, had carefully extracted a long piece of muscle from my lower calf, rotating it up over my knee and sewing it in place. The muscle graft is covered by a piece of skin harvested from the upper layer of my thigh. Inside, a zigzag of wires holds my knee together. My knee is a mass of raw skin and muscle, stapled in place to create a covering for the gaping hole that had been there before. Encased in bandages and a bulky knee brace, it engulfs me waves of pain when allowed to bend at all. I am warned to keep it immobilized, for now, to protect the grafts. My right ankle is enclosed in a plaster cast. I am a patchwork person, and the initial results of my refurbishment are even more painful than the original injuries.

I still need a considerable amount of help. Appallingly dependent, I cannot even stand up. My legs will no longer support me. I cannot so much as lift them off the bed; the muscles have atrophied so extensively. I cannot put weight on either leg. I am able to slide my way into a wheelchair only with considerable assistance. I cannot get up to use a toilet or a commode chair.

I tried to stand two days ago, with the help of my therapists and a walker, but could achieve only two short seconds before becoming so dizzy and nauseous that I had to lie down again. I wept bitter tears at my failure.

They say to allow seven to nine months for recovery. I should be able to walk, probably with a limp.

"You'd better get used to not doing everything you could before," says one doctor. I have no idea how extensive or how accurate that prediction is.

The hospital is unwilling to release me until my continuing care is assured. I will need ongoing medical treatment. I have an IV, now an internal tube inserted into my left arm that snakes through one of my veins and winds up near my heart. I will keep it for another month after I leave the hospital, providing for uninterrupted delivery of the harsh antibiotics that will hopefully prevent future recurrences of the pervasive infections that had taken hold during my time in the ravine.

The IV fluids would have to be renewed several times daily. My surgery sites will need fresh dressings. I am still ingesting Flagyl, the toxic medication meant to cure me of the intestinal ailment I picked up in the hospital. I have a prescription for Vicodin. I'll need it, they tell me. I'll have to come back to Fresno for a follow-up visit in a week or so, and I must then be passed into the hands of a capable local orthopedist who can make certain that my many broken bones are healing as they should. I will need extensive physical therapy.

Since I was brought in through the emergency room, the law requires that I be cared for, I have discovered. Although I have no health insurance, my hospital care will continue as long as I am at UMC, my bills continuing to mount. I've been told they are already over $250,000. There is not much I can do about that, so I try not to think of it. I have filled out a Medi-Cal application, but it has not yet been reviewed. Privately, I doubt that I will get any help. Too poor to afford health insurance, yet too well off to qualify for help, I am in that no-man's land between affluence and poverty.

When I leave the hospital, medical care will no longer be assured. I will be simply another sickly person with no ability to pay. I will have to provide funding for any additional treatment up front.

It has taken a team of friends many hours to arrange for my outpatient care, and to secure my release.

Where will I go? I cannot go home. I cannot yet be alone. I cannot care for myself, cannot get groceries or cook, cannot drive, cannot even stand up to walk to the toilet. I am unable to work, and will be for months. I do not qualify for public assistance of any sort, no workers' compensation, no unemployment, and no supplemental income of any kind. I have an IV in my arm that needs daily tending. I have no money to stay in an extended care facility, and no health insurance.

"Don't let them put me in a nursing home," I begged Carla in a semi-lucid moment during her first visit to the hospital. I fantasized about my large red-haired friend picking me up in her strong arms and running with me to safety. To where? I don't know. I don't remember my words later, but Carla does not forget.

Now she does not balk. She begins turning her little house into a rest home for me. The word goes out. Donations flood in, from word of mouth and from e-mail communities. People send money, hospital equipment, and potluck dishes. They contribute a hospital bed, a mattress, two walkers, a commode chair, a bathtub handle, and two wheelchairs. Carla's home fills with invalid equipment. Friends volunteer to move in a huge chest freezer to hold the food contributions, and to rearrange the furniture in Carla's office to make room for me, since she doesn't have an extra bedroom.

They find an orthopedist who is willing to accept me as a patient. Most of the doctors contacted are reluctant. My injuries are too complex, my ability to pay too undefined. After considerable exploration, Carla and Eddie are able to find Dr. Miles, a local MD who is willing to take my case on the faint assurance of eventual payment. His receptionist has read about me in the paper, and is intrigued by my story.

The Sutter Visiting Nurses Association (VNA), specializing in training people to do in-home care, will come to Carla's home and teach two friends to change my IV. Upon hearing the designation "self-pay," they agree to reduce their fees, and visit just once a week. We will be given a number to a twenty-four-hour hotline, should anything go wrong. Our friend Scott is an RN, and he promises to watch over the process as well. Delivery of IV drugs and additional wound dressing is arranged.

We calculate that it will cost us about $5,000 to $10,000 to spring me. The IV drugs alone are $1,200 a week; the visiting nurses who will help us cost several hundred. I will have to pay out of pocket for all other drugs, doctor's visits, x-rays, an ongoing Vicodin prescription, any additional surgery, and for physical therapy.

Donations from friends pay for the first installment of the visiting nurses bill and the expensive pharmaceuticals that will be pumped into my arm for another month.

The plan has come together. I am to be released. It is an amazing undertaking. Who are we to think that we can produce the complex package that is needed for my care? Who are we, an eclectic group of eccentrics, to imagine that we can somehow provide the treatment and the expertise and the certainty that is needed to create the next miracle, to restore me to the life I had almost lost. Who are we?

One thing that my friends have in common is a refusal to believe in the impossible. For the impossible is the undertaking of "Helping Amy." Here we are, a desperately injured woman with no health care coverage, and a group of people with a scant amount of conventional medical training, hardly any money, and precious little knowledge about financial assistance, or about how to care for an invalid at all. What we do have is a great deal of heart, and a lot of determination. Surely if any of us had stepped back and looked at the big picture, we would have seen that my restoration was not feasible, that we could not conceivably be doing what we had set out to do.

But nobody did that. Nobody voiced the doubt. All gave what they could, and somehow through faith and sweat and love and the miracle of ordinary people believing that they can create something extraordinary by simply helping one another, it all comes together. This is the miracle of HelpingAmy.

The plan has been implemented. The day of my departure is here. We have arranged to rush me from Fresno to Carla's home, where the recovery room has been set up, and where a nurse from the VNA will meet us to help install the first of many bags of infection-controlling antibiotics. The timing is important. We have just five hours to make the trip, needing to arrive at Carla's before my IV runs out.

I cannot sit in a car. My right leg will not bend at all, and I am in way too much pain to tolerate the jouncing of highway traffic for long. The only way to transport me is by ambulance, or, as my friends have arranged, in a padded van.

Lou, Coleen, and Adrian arrive at the hospital at 8 A.M., having gotten up at three to be there at the appropriate time. Reassuringly, Coleen has been a med tech in Colorado, accustomed to riding in an ambulance with severely wounded people. She is prepared with food, beverages, and calm reassurance to see to my every need.

The ambulance is Lou's roomy van, usually used to transport audio equipment for his business. Today, it is tricked out in the lush bohemian style that is my friends' trademark, all decorated in purple. It is rigged up for maximal comfort, with foam mattresses several layers thick padding the back. Purple velvet and brocade cushions are piled on either side, handy for propping me up in whatever way should be the most comfortable. Anxious as I am, this indication of the thoughtful care of my friends and the reminder of the colors of the world does much for my sagging confidence.

What would have become of me, had I not had my friends? I met a woman in the hospital, when I was finally able to get around the corridors in a wheelchair. Her injuries were very similar to mine. She had fallen down a flight of steps outside of her apartment. She, like me, had nobody at home to care for her. She had been in Fresno for two months, now staying at the extended care facility.

"You do not want to be there," she tells me with resignation. She herself has no choice. She has been befriended by an elderly man who comes from time to time to visit a relative. He will bring her burgers from McDonald's restaurant and the occasional pack of cigarettes. That is the best she has to look forward to.

My own assorted group of friends has banded together to care for me and carry me off. I sign final papers, and am wheeled out on a gurney, and slid gently into the purple ambulance. Lou drives, Coleen rides shotgun, and Adrian sits in back and holds my hand. I'm on my way to Carla's.

Amy and Carla in the purple ambulance. August 30, 2003.

28

At Carla's

Blessed with a strong immune system, I had usually managed to avoid even the colds and influenzas common to most people's experience. Now I am sick as a dog. Confined to a hospital bed, I ache in every limb, especially both legs. Physically devastated from the aftereffects of the injuries, repeated surgeries and ongoing antibiotic infusions, nauseous from continuing Flagyl medication, I am as ill as I've ever been in my life.

Vastly relieved to be out of the hated hospital, for I did hate it, despite my gratitude and relief, I find I have a new string of problems. I still need prodigious amounts of help. I am no longer surrounded by health care professionals. I still have to use a bedpan, and am immoderately embarrassed to have to ask one of my friends to take it away for me. Carla and Adrian are trained to change my IV once a day, a bag of fluids parked in a fanny pack and run by a timing device, hooked up to a nozzle at the end of the tube that has been shoved into my left upper arm.

Help continues to flood in. Single friends make a Welcome Home banner to commemorate my survival. "Our hero," it says. "Still seven lives left." Lory O. brings a wooden box that she has made herself, containing a sewing kit and other essentials. "Amy's Mending" proclaims the engraving on the top. People send herbal extracts, supplements, massage oils and tinctures. They volunteer acupuncture, hands-on healings, Integrated Awareness sessions, shamanic healings, Reiki work, massage and facials. They contribute checks and cash and prayers and stamps and cards and e-mails. Lauri Z. makes teeth for a living. She makes me a beautiful tooth to replace the one that snapped off during the impact of the fall. Linda organizes an ongoing meal delivery at Carla's home, complete with a calendar on the HelpingAmy Yahoo! Group's web site. Dinner is catered by a different friend each night. The freezer fills with casseroles. Lani loans a van for the trip back to Fresno. Everyone helps in whatever way they can.

At some time during my healing, my son, Sam, staying then with his dad, Big Sam, has a disagreement and runs away. Happily for all of us, he runs to Carla's. Now she has not just an invalid, but an extra teenager as well.

I am immensely glad to be here, and not in a nursing home, but Carla's home is not really very invalid friendly. She has a small duplex with tiny rooms and sharp corners, 1,200 square feet of space, just the right size for one woman and a boy. I have been installed in what was the office, since there is no extra guest room. There are little rugs everywhere, handy for tripping on, a tiny kitchen, steps at both doors, two cats and a dog. Carla and Daniel still have their busy lives to lead in and around my bedridden presence.

Already pressed for time, they arise each day at six and scurry to get ready for work and school, not to return home again until evening.

Amy and her son, Sam, at Carla's, September 2003.

Carla makes me breakfast before she takes off, calls often, and checks to make sure I will not be alone.

Life as a convalescent is hectic. The flow of visitors goes on and on. A different friend or group of friends brings dinner and sometimes lunch each day, all vying to see who can produce the tastiest meal. I need feeding. I weigh less than 120 pounds when I leave the hospital, not attractively slender, but looking more like a war victim, skin hanging prune-like over fleshless bone. I pretend appetite when I still have none, but I am genuinely glad to see my friends. The cumulative delight in my resurrection is unguarded and very real.

Sally and Francesca and Adrian are often there, Sally running about doing errands, Francesca asking insightful questions, and Adrian doing whatever he can to make the situation more livable, fixing something here, rearranging something there. He changes my bedpan or IV if Carla is not around.

I have no time to relax, and read, and allow my body to heal in peace and quiet. There is no leisure to process all that has happened to me. The Medi-Cal people want vast amounts of paperwork before they can review my case. I've already been turned down once. Still in the hospital, I missed the first deadline. My financial life is not easy to explain, since I am self-employed. Because I left home for just a short vacation, intending to go back to work when I returned, my affairs are in a shambles. I still cannot stand enough to get into my own house. Adrian has brought four large boxes of papers from my home, and I spend hours each day working on completing my tax returns, organizing my business records, and producing copies of all current expenses. I sit propped in my donated hospital bed and plug away, one stack of papers at a time. I am, by now, about $280,000 in debt.

Growing concerned about my pool card business, I help with that as well. I sit in bed and fold boxes and shipping cartons, stacking them up in piles around my wounded legs.

My world becomes more social than it has ever been. Friends come and go through the front and back doors; I am rarely alone. This is both a comfort and a trial to me, a person who likes living solo, and customarily seeks solitude as a panacea for the busyness of life. My life has become public knowledge. Everyone knows my story; I have been questioned and interviewed and documented. The details of my life, my daily habits, my financial affairs, my personal emotions, all are known now by scores of people. I am no longer a private person. I am here on display for all who wish to see me, still too much in need to protest.

People who have had serious injuries themselves seem particularly affected by my tale. They come to share their own stories, to commiserate, and to tell of their recovery. I welcome such stories. I need them, in those days, to encourage myself. Other than the estimate of seven to nine months, nobody has told me how much renewal I might expect with my newly created knee and patched together hip. I would always have a limp, they had told me regretfully in the hospital. But what did that mean? Would I hobble about, leaning on a cane or a crutch? I cannot picture myself as I had once been, hiking, running, laughing in the sunshine. I cannot imagine being whole again.

I lie in my bed and collect up the stories of healing, listening with eager ears. These people have gotten better, and so might I. The people themselves seem to need to tell of their experiences, to recall the trauma and the pain, but especially to remind themselves of the good fortune of survival and recovery.

Amy with walker.

As I grow more invested in regaining my mobility, Carla puts out a call at the physical therapy office where she works. Is anyone willing to volunteer their time to see me, still housebound as I am? John J. volunteers, and also Maria. Eddie Rosen makes a house call himself.

Maria comes first. Maria is small and slender, with a quiet demeanor and soft curly hair framing a sweet face. I like her immediately. I have worked for days to be able to ease both legs, the right still in a huge brace, inch by inch to the side of the bed, gently lowering each leg, and resting my feet tentatively on the floor. Now I show Maria what I can do, working myself slowly around to perch hesitantly on the side of the bed.

"And now stand up," says the gentle Maria with complete certainty. I know I can't stand up. I have not stood up unassisted since I crashed to the rock. Even with the aid of a walker, I can barely drag myself to a stand.

Hearing only the clarity of Maria's voice, I forget all of my fear and weakness and doubt.

"And now stand up." And so I do. Triumphantly, I push myself up off the bed, and unassisted, I come to a stand. Struggling that day to make only twenty steps, I clutch the walker with each one, until I am so sick and dizzy that I need to be wheeled back to bed. But it is enough. I can stand!

John J. comes often to see me at Carla's. He has infinite patience, working me step by step through elaborate processes. He trains me to be able to stand enough to use a commode chair, a toilet-like contraption that sits near the bed. We move it gradually farther and farther away until it lodges in the bathroom. Finally! I can toddle with my walker to the bathroom, almost like a real person.

Best of all is the day, about three weeks after I get to Carla's, when I can first go outside. We work long and hard that day, John and I, step by step, motion by motion, for I must not be allowed to fall and re-injure myself—an imminent possibility. We maneuver the walker around corners and through doorways, across treacherous rugs, over the door sill, onto the landing, and, most difficult of all, down two shallow steps. I almost give up; arms quaking, body teetering, I almost can't make it. But finally, here I am, standing on the sidewalk, in the sunshine, in front of Carla's house. John hovers nearby, ready to be of immediate assistance should that prove necessary.

Recklessly, I release my iron grip on the walker and for one jubilant moment, I throw my arms up over my head in triumph.

"I'm out!"

It is the first time I've been able to get outside under my own steam since the Purple Ambulance delivered me to Carla's door. The ultimate triumph, the sweetness of victory snatched from the jaws of defeat, is mine.

29

Many Firsts

T here are many such firsts in the months to come. Each one carries with it fear, doubt, and then the ultimate joy of a goal achieved, a hardship conquered. Tiny pleasures are cherished: the first time I can inch my way into Carla's kitchen and raid the refrigerator, the first time I can go to the grocery store in my wheelchair and pick out food for myself. The first step, the first two successive steps. No small gain is trivial. I count the days as I slowly regain my mobility and then my autonomy.

Food is a big motivator. Always hungry these days, I need adequate nutrition to rebuild muscle I lost during long weeks of enforced inactivity. Vitamins and minerals will help my body with its extensive healing processes of cellular restructuring and nerve growth, restoring bone and tissue to health.

I am hungry as well for tastes of living. Every bite, each trifling experience is savored, as little by little, I remember and regain the details that together weave a life. A friend takes me to a movie. I can wear clothes other than hospital gowns. I can finally ease a pair of pants over my stiff legs. My feet are too swollen for shoes, but I find a pair of slippers that will do. I wash my own hair in the bathroom sink. No victory is too small for celebration, no pleasure too trivial for acknowledgment in these early days. Each tiny gift or chore completed is a first, to be appreciated and treasured. I am always eager to recover more of my autonomy, and never far from the memory that I almost didn't have a life at all.

Adrian, understanding my intense desire to expand the boundaries past the limited scope that has become my world, is often there for the firsts.

Midgley's Country Flea Market in Sebastopol is a sprawling outdoor market heaped with miscellaneous used treasures of all descriptions. A bargain hunter's delight, Midgley's opens up every Saturday and Sunday morning at 6:30 A.M. During these rough days of recuperation at Carla's, one if my greatest pleasures is to go to the flea market. Adrian arrives at Carla's at six. Since I still cannot bend or flex enough to dress myself, he swaddles me in sweatpants and fleeces, piles me into my wheelchair, maneuvers me down the steps to the car, then loads me in; the complicated process requires a wheelchair, a walker, and multiple pillows. Arms straining, I scootch myself carefully into the backseat, sitting crosswise. My leg still will not bend enough to get into the front seat. At Midgley's, we reverse the painstaking process. Just getting there takes about an hour and a half. Adrian wheels me across the rough ground in my chair, past tables of dusty merchandise, where I bargain enthusiastically. I sift through stacks of booty with the help of a long metal grabber that I've been given to help me reach things during my convalescence. Starved as I am for mobility,

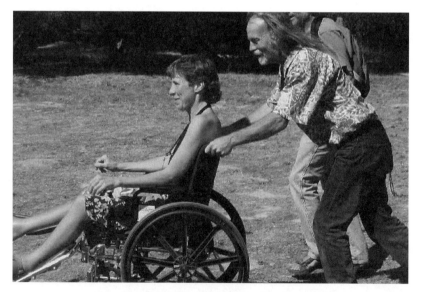

Amy in wheelchair with Adrian, October 2003.

for shopping, for any taste of life, these mornings are the delight of my invalid existence. Adrian never once complains about the time and the effort.

It is the end of September. I want to go home. I haven't been home since mid-July. Living at Carla's for a month now, I know that she will do anything for me, but tension has built during the difficult weeks. At first a much-needed haven for me, Carla's home has become a busy place that is not a refuge for either one of us. We both crave more solitude.

On the first of October, my forty-seventh birthday, I move back home. I'm cast and brace and medication free. I still cannot drive, or cook, or do many household chores. I have to spend long hours with my legs propped up to reduce the swelling that may cause circulation damage if not controlled. Walking, still only with a walker, is a painful process requiring both hands and considerable focused concentration. A few trips to my own kitchen and bathroom are about what I can handle in any one day. Going home brings with it the same exultation and terror that I felt when leaving the hospital. But I relish the peace and quiet, being in my own home, surrounded by my own things, with my cats and my son.

Amy at Midgley's Flea Market, September 2003. Photo by Adrian Morgan.

I still have many visitors. HelpingAmy continues. Laurie B. cleans my house. Her husband, Dave, sends Tachyon herbal tinctures and Lauri Z. climbs a ladder and clears out the storm gutters for me. John donates a bed; I was accustomed to a futon but cannot lower myself onto it now. Wendy replants my front yard, gone to weed after months of neglect. My sister, Ellen, sends a collection of videos all the way from Boston. Sam has stocked up on chicken soup, having read in the paper that I like it. He prepares meals, fetches things, mows the lawn, and carries out the trash, all without being reminded. My neighbor ,Luisa, limping herself from a recent leg injury, takes me to the store for groceries. Amy's Kitchen, a natural foods company based in Sonoma County, contributes three cases of frozen organic dinners. Adrian moves in the new mattress and installs a shower nozzle, since I can't maneuver myself to sit down in the bathtub. He and Francesca continue as frequent visitors.

Being home provides a whole new wave of challenges, but also a new round of firsts. Customary chores, once an impediment to the life I wanted to be living, become joyful markers of continuing recovery. I can do a load of laundry. I can unload my dishwasher, with the help of a wheeled walker, and my grabber. I can wear shoes.

The world is filled with firsts.

30

Many Heroes

There are many heroes in my tale. Certainly my three Buddhist angels must be counted among them, and the team of rescue rangers, the men who drove the helicopters, the firefighters from Reedley, and the magnificent surgeons and staff from UMC in Fresno. Carla and the many people of "Helping Amy" are also counted among my own personal saviors. Of all the heroes in my story, one of the finest and the least recognized is Eddie Rosen. It is Eddie who restores to me the quality of the life that I love.

Eddie is Carla's boss. He owns a physical therapy office, Physical Therapy and Movement Education Center (PTMEC) in Cotati, about forty-five minutes from where I live. Eddie and I have had a warm but occasional acquaintance. When he learns that his office manager has gone to visit me in the hospital, he accepts her sudden absence without protest. When he hears my story, he doesn't hesitate.

First he visits me himself at Carla's house, assessing my need for postoperative rehabilitation.

"Bring her in," he tells Carla. As soon as I am able to travel, eased crosswise into the backseat of my car, I am transported to his PTMEC as a pathetic bundle of pulverized bones and loose skin, muscles almost nonexistent, flesh hanging on my now puny body. Eddie, a gifted and skilled therapist, appraises my condition himself.

Eddie knows I cannot pay. I have no insurance, and no money. I am now about $300,000 in debt, and I still cannot walk. I can hardly stand. The amount of restoration that will be needed to get me functional again is immense. He has Carla book me into his PTMEC office for two hours each day, using all of his highly trained therapists. I am welcome at the office at any time, to do additional work in the gym or the therapeutic hot pool.

Eddie never says a word to me about this tremendous gift. I know what a bequest it is; I do the math in my head. He personally pays his therapists to care for me.

I also know what an amazing gift is the ability to walk again, and to walk well. This is the sort of blessing that no amount of money can buy. I am getting far more care than patients with health insurance are usually allotted.

The only thing required of me is that I show up when scheduled, and be willing to work. I do this with all the energy I have available to me, coming early, staying late, putting in three to four hours of physical therapy a day, working to exhaustion, and sometimes beyond. Dedicated to not letting this godsend go to waste, I never miss an appointment.

When I move back home at the beginning of October, I am fairly mobile within my own space. Now that I have the go-ahead from my doctors for full weight bearing, as tolerated, and bending, if possible, the quality of my future life depends upon how hard I'm willing to work and how often I can get to Eddie's PT office.

I cannot drive to my appointments. The bus takes two hours one way. I send out a message to the HelpingAmy Yahoo! group, asking for rides to physical therapy.

My friends rally again. Together, they contribute to an amazing and creative transportation effort. Every weekday, for a solid month, a different friend shows up to drive me the forty-five minutes to physical therapy. Each day someone picks me up at PTMEC and takes me home again. Everyone who can help gives generously, driving my car or theirs, making time from their own busy lives, sometimes bringing their kids with them or fitting me in between jobs and other errands. Sam's dad volunteers, and so do my neighbors. Often my helpers come early or stay late to visit and assist with chores or errands. Once again I am overwhelmed by the care and concern that go into my resurrection, and by the love of the many people in my life.

"What do you want to be when you grow up?" Eddie asks me sometimes when he is working on me. It is a joke of his. He, at around my age, is still pondering that question for himself.

"I don't want to grow up," I tell Eddie. We agree that being grown up implies some sort of a stopping place. Neither one of us wants that.

"What do you want to be *while* you're growing up?" amends Eddie. I know what I want to be while I'm growing up. I want to be like Eddie. I want to be someone who bestows the blessings of my skills upon those who need them without a selfish thought, without any consideration of gain or reward. I want to be able to transform people's existence, to restore them to themselves, to bring the light back into their lives, the way that Eddie is doing for me.

31

Like a Junkyard Dog

I think of him as Doctor Smiley, although he doesn't smile much. His gravity reflects his concern for my future. Dr. Miles is the orthopedist to whom I have been assigned upon my release from the hospital. I am grateful that he is willing to take my case. My bones seem to be repairing well. "Work like a junkyard dog," is Dr. Miles' advice. He seems to believe in progress through challenge rather than through encouragement. Perhaps his technique works.

Whatever the instigation—my own tough determination, my desire to coax a smile from Dr. Miles, or my wish to make all of my therapists proud—I do just that: work like a junkyard dog. I devote myself entirely to physical rehabilitation. Nothing is more important to me than learning to walk again.

My physical condition is riddled with complications. My skin is peeling off in big flaky portions, probably a side effect of the many rounds of antibiotics. My feet still swell alarmingly, creating possible circulatory problems, and susceptibility to infection. My right lower leg is so numb from nerve damage that I can hardly move my toes. The piece of calf muscle newly grafted over my knee seems confused as to its new location. A light touch on my knee brings muscle spasms and cramps shooting through my calf. Both legs are so weak that I cannot so much as lift either one.

The left hip, right knee, and right foot are so badly damaged that they leave me with no semblance of a normal walk. Neither leg can be relied upon. Both must be retrained simultaneously. I am constantly in danger of falling, or of compensating with other parts of my body, and tweaking out my back, my one good hip, or some other uninjured portion.

One of the most prohibitive problems is the inflexibility of my right knee and ankle, both having been casted for close to a month and now frozen in position. Without a normal range of motion, I will not be able to walk smoothly, climb steps, or perform the usual tasks that legs are required to do. To bend the joints requires me to literally rip through the scar tissue that holds them locked in place.

I become a slave to the goniometer, a clinical device that measures range of motion. I fight for each painful degree, counting them the way a miser counts gold, activating the same determination that got me scootching down that ravine. I measure the success of my days by the amount that I can bend my knee. As I force the leg to bend, one tortuous degree at a time, I must also build up muscle strength to complement the new range of motion.

The weeks pass in a blur. Getting ready, getting to PT, working for two hours each day with a trained therapist, then working in the gym for another hour or two consumes all of my energy. I manage to make it home, and that's it. Sam and I eat whatever is around, food from the freezer, TV dinners, sandwiches brought by friends from the grocery store. I cannot work, or socialize, or even do my own errands and chores. I never have the leisure time that people imagine is the luxury possessed by the semi-invalid. They visualize me reclining; using my many hours of down time to read, write, perhaps make phone calls. I do none of those things. Every iota of energy I have is spent on PT. I push myself to the max each day, crying often with defeat and exhaustion. I should be doing more. I should be doing better.

Eddie Rosen's staff is highly skilled and varied in their approach. Sylvia retrains my body with Feldenkrais Method sessions. John works patiently on balance and mobility training, emphasizing functional orientation. Barbara, having recovered from serious injury herself, shares her determination while teaching me the Pilates method of movement education, using the original movement equipment: the Reformer, the Cadillac and the Chair. Mary, always with an encouraging word, works closely with Barbara in the Pilates gym. Lori B., also a working mother and an athlete, pushes my range of motion, and is full of practical suggestions about how to incorporate PT into regular life.

All of Eddie's staff are trained in body mechanics and alignment. I experience a diversity of neuromuscular aquatic therapies in the therapeutic hot pool, and a variety of joint and soft tissue mobilizations and massage. They put me to work using exercise balls, tennis balls, elastic stockings, stretchy bands and steps. I do floor exercises, table exercises, door exercises and pool exercises. I do laps around the PT office with walker or crutches, and practice climbing stairs, one bend at a time. I learn pelvic rolls and foot flexes and side steps and one-legged stands. I work on strength and balance, muscle elongation, increased elasticity, and lateral and medial ranges of motion. My therapists give forth a wealth of ideas and encouragement.

Despite my immense gratitude, these are some of the most difficult days of my life. I am always exhausted; my body aches constantly. I counter my desires to avoid hurt and coerce myself into allowing even more pain, a necessary ingredient if I am to regain normal function. I live on the verge of despair much of the time, and every day I push myself farther that I think I can go. I never know ultimately how much better I can get, how much of my old strength and flexibility I can regain. Probably no one else does either. There is no time for me to acknowledge the pain and the fear. And there is no room for doubt. As in the ravine, doubt is a luxury I cannot afford.

By the end of September, I have forced my knee into a paltry thirty-degree bend. I can stand and walk about ten yards clutching my walker.

"What are your goals?" The therapists always ask new patients. "I want to climb Half Dome again," I tell them.

In October, I begin PT at the office, wheeled in that first day in a wheelchair. A little bit at a time, I increase my walking range, toddling slowly down the hallway with my walker, a cluster of therapists eyeballing my every move, correcting the nuances of my gait, cheering me on, and bragging about me to the other clients. A week or so later, for the first time since the fall, I am able to take a few faltering but unassisted steps. Primeval woman could not have been more pleased to discover the possibilities of walking on two legs. A toddler could not be more triumphant when standing upright for the first time. I store up the joy of the moment, a few footfalls closer to glimmers of hiking yet to come.

By October tenth, I can walk once around the block with my walker. By the twentieth, I gain a sixty-degree bend. I am introduced to crutches. I work toward walking a half mile with crutches, and navigating necessary places like grocery stores and post offices, a daypack on my back to carry essentials. The entire staff of the Healdsburg Post Office comes out to cheer when I make it in for the first time.

By the end of October, I am finally able to drive. Probably I shouldn't be on the road just yet. I can bend my leg enough to wedge myself into the driver's seat, but I have to hook my right hand under my knee to assist it in moving from gas to brake; it has not the strength or flexibility to make the motions on its own. I drive myself to PT each day, a round trip of fifty miles, carefully down the back roads. I'm clutching my knee and moaning in pain as I pull up at home, right foot totally numb with swelling. I wrestle my crutches out of the backseat, and hobble into the house. The trip depletes my small store of strength. But the day when I can first drive my car is one of the happiest days I can ever remember.

My knee still will not bend into a right angle. Dr. Miles insists that I must make ninety by the end of November, or he will consider "manipulation under anesthesia." That sounds ominous. I work still harder.

Despite the constant struggle, I am happy during these weeks, as each day brings me a little closer to recovery. I dub Eddie's Physical Therapy office "Club Amy," to keep up my morale. I park a swimsuit there, and make good use of the hot pool. I develop an undying passion for sushi, and indulge myself relentlessly. Raw fish seems to be just what my mending body craves. I treat myself to sushi every day, hobbling across the street on crutches to get a little plastic tray of carryout.

On November fourth, three months since the fall, I am promoted from crutches to hiking poles. Eddie has wisely suggested the change. The poles will give me a more normal gait, and even more importantly, I feel like a hiker again, not an invalid. I treat myself to a brand new pair of titanium trekking poles, to replace the one still stuck in a tree in a ravine near the Tehipite Valley.

All of the health professionals agree that I'm way ahead of the curve as far as recovery is concerned. Nevertheless, I have no energy for anything else. Both of my legs hurt much of the time. I still need my Vicodin prescription to coax my limbs through the painful experiences that will restore them to their full range of usefulness.

On November twelfth, we measure an eighty-three-degree bend. By mid-November, I am able to climb a ladder to Adrian's boat, currently in dry dock. Only about twelve feet off the ground, but suddenly overcome by fear of the height, I tremble in every limb. But I make it to the top. By the end of November, I am put to practicing on flights of stairs, still a challenge for my bend-resistant knee. Much to my delight, I can claim a ninety-degree flexion, but only with my therapist Lori B. sitting on my leg. Ninety degrees means I can regain a normal walk, climb steps, fit into theater seats, and sit in most cars. Hooray!

In early December, Dr. Miles measures only eighty degrees, and warns me that I won't ever regain full range. I work harder. By mid-December, I have a bend of one hundred, and can do a half-mile on the treadmill, with a little arm support. I still can't bend my legs enough to get a complete rotation on the stationary bicycle, so I do 1,000 back-and-forths each day. By the end of December, I can at last pedal all the way round on the stationary bike, with a bend of 114. My car-driving range is up to 120 miles in a day, and I even feel safe to drive in rush hour traffic.

My therapists scan my every move, on the lookout for pelvic rotation, faulty heel placement, foot pronation, hip imbalance, and any other compensation for weakness or lack of bend. Mere mobility is not enough for my therapists. They want me to walk perfectly. I want that too.

In January, almost five months since the fall, I can walk with my trusty poles to the Healdsburg Plaza and back again, a two-mile round trip from my home. Afterwards I'm as tired as if I'd climbed a high mountain pass, and as pleased. My therapists and I spend January increasing the range of motion, and fine-tuning my gait. At the end of the month, Adrian takes me to Lake Tahoe, to the northern part of mountains that I love, where I am delighted to be able to hike in snowshoes. I still feel the weakness and the pain, but each week I can do new things.

In February, six months after the accident, my knee bends to 123 degrees; 130 will bring me to within the normal range of motion. Ever my own harshest critic, I chafe at ongoing limitations, and criticize myself when my gait falls below par. By mid-February I can walk four level miles on a bike path. My therapists design a special Pilates exercise that we dub "Climbing Half Dome." I obtain a rebounder, so I can work at home on more subtle types of motion.

I'm doing exceptionally well, my therapists tell me. I've become the poster child for the office. They point me out to other clients. Most of the other patients don't have injuries as serious as mine. Many feel sorry for themselves. It's a rare patient who can hold onto their own measure of self-pity once they have heard my story. I set out to cheer up and inspire the other patients. I figure it's the least I can do for my PT office.

I am reunited with my three rescuers. They are delighted to see me walking about. Jake gives me a gift; the very same whistle that he had carried in the ravine, and used to signal me. I remember how much

Amy on snowshoes. Photo by Adrian Morgan.

Amy reunited with her three wilderness angels. Left to right:
Adrian, Amy, Walter, Leslie, and Jake. Photo by Adrian Morgan.

Amy and Jake's whistle with Jake in the background,
March 2004. Photo by Adrian Morgan.

hope I had assigned to those two tiny toots, that desolate afternoon in the ravine, as I enfold the whistle tightly in my hand.

I am cut back to only three days a week of PT. My knee bend is up to 125 degrees. No longer content with level walking, I set the treadmill on a slant. On days off, I seek out hills for my daily walks. I continue on the Pilates machines. I take a holiday, and drive with my son in his rickety 1968 Chevelle to Seattle, to visit my brother Dan and his wife Kelly. Friends consider this quite an adventure.

In April, after eight months of repair and rehabilitation, I can finally ride my street bicycle. Determined to backpack again, but still tentative on steep grades, I plan in May for my first backpacking trip, in Henry W. Coe State Park, near Morgan Hill. I habitually go there each spring, loving it for its beauty as well as the ruggedness of its terrain. This time, I take Adrian with me for help and support. It is a very special moment when I lace up my hiking boots and swing my pack onto my back for the first time since the fall. My pack weighs about twenty pounds. We are light of step and light of heart. We hike for four days, completing a short twelve-mile loop with a 2,400-foot elevation change. Sometimes exhausted, often exultant, I feel stronger and healthier than I have since the fall. The aches are the remembered ones that come as a natural part of backpacking, not the less welcome pains of healing bones and weakened muscles. I'm still a long way from those 120-mile loops, but this trip is a huge step for me in body and spirit. What a blessing it is to be alive, and to be hiking again in the wilderness.

In mid-May, nine months after the fall, I am decreed well enough to graduate from PT. Other people need the services of Eddie and his dedicated staff more than I. Ecstatic at this fruition, I am also as fearful as a child leaving home for the first time. Will I continue to heal without the daily support of my cadre of therapists? PTMEC has become like a home to me, in these many months. I always know where I can go for encouragement, advice, conversation and concern. Now I am cast out, to be alone with my ongoing recovery. The PTMEC staff assures me that I am welcome at the office and in the gym anytime. But I know this is the end of an extraordinary epoch. These have been some of the worst and some of the best days of my life.

I embrace my new freedom. In July, I hike often in the hills around home, climbing steep fire roads, not without pain and effort, but with great joy. I am out in the world again, and I can once again walk about, almost as I used to.

People on the street can hardly tell there is anything wrong. My therapists and I have worked so hard that on most days I do not show even the predicted limp.

"Skin your knee?" inquires one solicitous man, spying my scar, revealed by a pair of shorts. If only he knew. Even close friends assume that I am all healed up, just the same as I always was. I still feel keenly my own weaknesses and limitations and watch anxiously for signs of continuing healing. They are still to be found. And celebrated. I still find those firsts in almost every day.

I can scamper jauntily up and down steps, almost as I used to. I open my Everyday Goddess business again, lifting around heavy bins of clothing, and having fun dancing about and dressing my friends. I can swim again. Can I slide on the waterslide? I can! I maneuver my way through crowds of people, turning nimbly sideways and easing my way through the traffic flow. Not long ago, I could not have done

Amy at Point Reyes, hiking again, August 2004. Photo by Adrian Morgan.

that, unsteady as I was with my newly learned gait. I feel like a hiker again as I glide swiftly past slower folk. I have regained my long loping stride. I can hike five miles, seven, and finally ten. Another first, another reclamation, another cause for personal jubilation. Spontaneously, I buy a plane ticket for three weeks in Asia next October. Will I be up to the trip? I'll find out. The firsts continue to flow, and each one floods me with gratitude. No single step is taken for granted. I savor the many sweetnesses of my life, as bit by bit my independence is returned to me.

32

The Questions

As I work my way toward physical recovery, my mind slowly releases the trauma stored within, offering up the opportunity for emotional healing, one piece at a time. I have occasional flashbacks to the ill-fated day that I fell into the ravine. There are still things that I don't understand, questions I want to ask.

How did this happen?

A cautious and experienced hiker, I take care where I place my feet, and I use particular vigilance in tricky situations. I was well-focused and alert on that afternoon. Time and time again I relive the motion of that final step. I am holding on with both hands, reaching out my foot, feeling safe and certain, then suddenly I am falling. It was the right foot that led the way, the right foot that reached out toward solid ground and found only the void. It was the right foot that hit the rock first, turning under, bending beneath the weight of my fallen body. A year later, my foot is still partially numb. I can hardly bear for anyone to touch it. The emotion stored within that foot is still too raw.

The emotions are complex: pain and terror, anger at myself for not somehow foreseeing the fall and preventing it, anger at the foot for leading the way into disaster. I am grateful to that limb as well, for making the sacrifice, and taking the brunt of the fall. I carry hidden within me a deep regret, and also a feeling of betrayal.

Was I betrayed?

Before the accident, I was accustomed to regarding gravity as a friend.

"It's the earth's way of giving you a hug," someone had told me once, and I had adopted that image. I felt myself to be safe as I hiked along in the embrace of our planet, and then suddenly I was not. I recall the way my stomach roiled as I felt all that was certain in the world drop out from under me. I am engulfed again by my own despair. The earth itself has betrayed me. As I fall through the air, gravity becomes a death threat, not a friendly acquaintance. The treachery cuts deep, damaging my trust in the physical safety of life.

The loss of my ability to stand also affected me deeply. It seemed to me a primordial right, and also a personal one. The ability to walk on two legs has belonged to humankind since before recorded history. I had earned my own right to walk as a toddler. For me, loving my mobility, walking means exploration, adventure, autonomy, security, and the safety promised by potential flight from danger. I had known the joy of locomotion, confident and strong, my determined strides meaning so much. Hundreds of vigilant steps, thousands of steady footfalls, and then one step, one millisecond, one footfall that denies me all of this, snatches away my rights, and changes everything.

Did I create this?

I live in a part of the world where self-determination is a popularly accepted belief. People like to suppose that we create what happens to us. I too have sometimes believed this, especially when all is going well. Willing to take pride in my creations, I find it comforting to think that some manifestation of mine has led to my good fortune.

It is easy for those of us who are relatively privileged to adopt a belief in self-creation. Naturally we want to congratulate ourselves for our prosperity. Of course we want to believe that we are deserving. And better still, that we can ensure the continuation of our blessings. It is prudent to feel pride of creation, if one is fortunate.

With it all comes the presumption of control. If we have created, we can create again, and what we are creating, we can master.

These beliefs shattered as I felt myself plummeting through the air. The few seconds of total helplessness that marked my fall had a profound effect upon how I perceive my role in the determination of my own fate. Freefall became the ultimate lesson in humility. I no longer believe myself to be always in control. I no longer entertain a secure belief in the malleability of circumstance, in self-determination, self-creation, and the illusion of being in charge of my destiny.

There may be times when we wield influence. Surely my decision to live had vital impact. But however much I desired a certain outcome, I cannot take credit for my salvation. Without the intervention of the miraculous, it would have made no difference. I would now be a pile of bones in the wilderness.

Nor do I claim responsibility for that horrible accident. I didn't want to break both of my legs. I don't want the pain and suffering. I don't embrace the physical weaknesses that will now always be a part of my life.

I look down at my legs, once the most beautiful part of me, long and strong and tanned. I see them now, scarred and cut and wrinkled and malformed. I remember being able to go and go indefinitely without exhaustion, effortlessly and joyfully, on those same legs. I shift my body a little and mutter a curse at the pain that is often a constant in my hip nowadays.

Maybe I am just too stubborn, too tough a case to understand these lessons and receive these gifts in any other way. I do not like to think so. I want to learn, but I would rather have had a gentler lesson.

Was there any warning?

Over and over I scan my consciousness. Was there a warning? Was there a moment when I knew I had a choice to make, and I took that step, chose that path, selected that motion instead of some other?

Often in my life, I have narrowly escaped disaster. In one particularly striking incident, I just missed the terrorist bombing on Bali in October 2002. If I had arrived there on the day that I intended, I could easily have been within range of the bombs. As it was, the airline flight I had chosen was full, and I was rescheduled to fly in just eleven hours after the blast.

I believed, even before the fall, that I have some sort of spiritual protection, some guidance, angels or spirit beings who watch over me, who protect me from harm. I also have a little voice in my head, a clear true voice that whispers direction. Other people have it too. They call it intuition, or guidance, or the voice of God. My voice tells me about things like drinks that will spill, items that will be left behind, and important bits of information that might be forgotten. It tells me what foods will make me sick, when to go or to stay, what person I must call today, which route to take. This voice is never wrong, and usually I obey it without hesitation. Occasionally I test the wisdom of the voice, through stubborn disagreement (I don't WANT to put down that chocolate cake) or through inattention. When I ignore the voice, I am always sorry.

I scour my memories. Did I, at any point prior to my fall, hear that little voice? Did I fail to notice it or choose to ignore it? Time and time again I reach the same conclusion. There was no voice. I had no warning.

Eight months after the accident, I go to see a psychic. I walk up the sidewalk to the porch of the small one-story house that is home to the Santa Rosa branch of the Berkeley Psychic Institute. Little has changed since I studied here, some seven years ago. Inside, it looks much like a regular home. Clairvoyant students are sitting about on folding chairs meditating, or standing up, giving aura healings to one another. Susan runs the Institute, and I have asked for a reading from her. We sit opposite each other in two of the chairs. She closes her eyes.

I want her to look clairvoyantly at my accident. She tells me what she sees, mostly validating what I already know. Finally I gain the courage to blurt out my most smoldering question.

It is difficult for me to ask. I force the words through reluctant lips. I have been hiding a deep resentment.

"Why did this happen to me?"

Why did this happen? It's not fair. Worse still, I secretly wonder if I am being punished for some unknown fault. Perhaps, I think in private, I am intrinsically bad, and I deserve this suffering.

Susan tells me simply that I was meant to have that experience, that I had been heading toward that place for several years. There was no way I could have avoided it, she says. I recall reading the words in William Tweed's book about the Tehipite and having a sudden deep desire to go to that very spot. She is right. I had been heading there for years. There is solace in the thought that it was meant to happen.

There is comfort, too, in what she says next. "There were angels with you in the ravine. They protected you so that you would come to no harm." I thank her, and go on my way.

Still searching for wisdom, I ask God, "Why me? Why did this have to happen?" I feel myself engulfed in a vast eternity of compassion. "It had to be so," is the message, as gentle as the touch of a butterfly's wing, as vast as the ocean, and as immutable as a mountain. "It had to be so." No more, and no less. It had to be so.

Perhaps it is not about me at all. Maybe I am just a cog in some bigger wheel, some piece of a greater plan. Who am I to claim the impact for myself alone? Who knows what reverberations my fall may have, what ripples my story may send out into the world. I am but a single person in a small moment. I like the thought that my misadventure could serve some higher purpose.

Oddly enough, I don't think to wonder why I was saved. That I am alive is blessing enough. Secure in the belief that I was spared for some reason, I am content not to know why. Purpose will unfold in its own time.

There is one more message for me. "You must tell the story," says that trusted little voice in my head. I listen to that voice, as I always try to do. And I begin to write the story.

33

After the Fall

In March, seven months after my fall, I am still faced with $300,000 in medical bills. During the long months of healing, I could not allow myself to lose hope by dwelling on the financial possibilities. Learning to walk was more important than anything.

Now I worry more about my monetary problems. Without any assistance, I know that I could lose everything, including my home and my livelihood. Collection agencies have started to call. I calculate that if I could somehow manage to pay $300 a month, it would take me eighty-three years to pay what I owe.

So as I go on learning to use my legs again, I also continue the lengthy process of reapplying for help from Medi-Cal. I have already supplied over 200 pages of varying documentation and been turned down twice. I still won't give up. I am assigned a new eligibility worker. After hearing the extent of my injuries, she suggests filing a special disaster assistance application: Medi-Cal for a limited period. I do as she suggests.

Finally, I receive word from Social Services. Due to the extreme nature of my hardship, I have been granted retroactive Medi-Cal for just one month, the month of August 2003. I was at UMC from August eighth until August thirtieth. About $11,000 is still my responsibility, but the other $289,000 is paid, through the grace of the California Department of Health Services.

I weep heartfelt sobs of helpless gratitude and incredible relief. This seems to me like the final miracle in my salvation. I am rescued from financial destruction. Surely the world is a hospitable place, if these kinds of miracles can happen, if people in hardship can receive help when they need it so desperately.

Like a mother measures the age of her newborn in moments, I count my own life from the time of the fall. At first, I counted each day. Days stretched into weeks, then months. Like an anxious parent, I watched myself as a helpless babe, not even capable of controlling my bowels, unable to stand erect on two legs. I cheered myself through my own toddler phase, and watched my transition back into the living, walking, able-bodied, grown human that I am.

Life is not as easy in many ways, and yet I am easier with it.

I do hold a new level of caution. I carry the memory of great pain, and I know the cost of error and injury. I fear falling, for myself and for others. I take care to protect my still-susceptible body from further harm. I shield my knee against sudden bumps. I avoid slippery places, side steps or unexpected jerky landings that might wrench my hip. I don't run or jump in my former carefree way. I cannot kneel, or sit with ease on the ground for long. I can hike ten miles now, but always with some discomfort. I dance reluctantly, knowing that future pain will be my payment for the temporary pleasure of motion. I gauge my stamina carefully, and am cautious not to strand myself in a place or situation that will take me past my still-measurable endurance. Some days my legs just hurt, and I give in to the need for rest.

I feel sorrow for my legs, for the loss of their strength and beauty. My legs have taken the brunt of the fall, those strong Irish legs, a gift from my mountain hiking ancestors, once the toughest part of me. I am immeasurably grateful for their sacrifice, but I mourn the mutilation, the devastation to my once-sturdy limbs, and also the loss of their beauty.

My legs will forever bear the scars. A three-by-four-inch patch of discolored skin marks my right thigh. An angry,` red twelve-inch gash slashes my left. My right calf has a permanent indentation in the back, and another surgical slash, from ankle to knee. The right knee is misshapen and discolored, with an abnormal blob of muscle tissue over the front, and a dark, four-by-six-inch scar that resembles a relief map of Australia. My legs have not regained the sleek muscle tone of previous years. They are dimpled and pocked with stressed and slackened skin. Once, people would cross the street to tell me what beautiful legs I had. Now, they glance and look away. Mini-skirts have become things of the past.

At the same time, I am proud of those scars. I did well to survive, and even better to recover as I have done. The scars are battle marks. They show the stuff of which I am made. I have earned my restoration, and my pride.

My scars remind me of the blessings of being alive, and the miracles that assisted me in that outcome. I cannot run my hand over my marked knee without immense gratitude. My legs: I still have them, and they work. Work well. I can hike again.

Some of my harsh edges have been softened, my aggressive drive smoothed down a bit. I move more slowly. The world is able to catch up. I watch hurrying people, pushing by me, impatient to be on their way, intolerant of those less capable. Was I ever that impatient? I hope not.

I am more content, more often, to take it easy. I cherish the rest break as much as the constant motion of a still-fascinating life. Friends are relieved because now they can keep up. I move at a better pace for them, more available now for mellow companionship. Death has almost caught up with me, and I have allowed life to catch up with me as well.

My measure of compassion has been expanded. I have known great suffering. I have lived the life of the ill and infirm, and in doing so have gained more understanding of the human experience. I feel for those in pain. I know now in a very personal way what people who have been injured are going through.

I have sympathy for those who have lost a limb. I myself came so very close. I have empathy for people who have a disability of some sort. I recall vividly the days when I was handicapped myself, and am grateful that, for me, it was only temporary. My handicapped parking permit expired in March 2004. I had quit using it weeks before anyway, leaving the parking spaces for people who needed them more than I. The red tag is still in my glove compartment. I keep it there to remind myself of how fortunate I am, and that now, it is only a souvenir.

I would like to be able to say that my miraculous survival resulted in an epiphany and that all of life is a delight. It is not always so. I still have bad times, the days when my personal Almira takes over. My legs ache, my computer doesn't work, my love life is in a shambles.

On those days, I tell myself a story, a tale of courage and fortitude and love and miracles and salvation. The story is a true one, and reminds me what a blessing even the worst of times can be.

34

Gifts and Revelations

L ife is more precious to me, and more defined, now that I have
seen it hanging in the balance.

My life itself is a gift. A life that was almost lost has been
found. Every experience that I have now is a bonus. Each moment of
continuation is to be celebrated, cherished, appreciated all the more for
having so nearly been taken away.

Before the fall, I sometimes felt unsure. Was living a good thing?
Was it worth going on at all? The seconds of the fall, the feeling of vast
disappointment when I was certain my time had come to an end, are
still fresh within my memory. The days I thought were my last are still
vivid. Clearest of all is the moment when I knew that I held my life to
be dear, with no ambivalence and no doubt. No amount of uncertainty
can stand up to that time in the ravine when I prayed for help, that
moment of clarity when I knew unequivocally. Yes. I want to live.

Another revelation is the recognition of exactly what I cherish in
my life. Looking back over the years from my vantage point at the bottom of the ravine, I had the opportunity to consider how I had spent
the hours of my existence, and which experiences were meaningful.
From that unique perspective, poised for a few days between life and
death, sorting through the sad times and the happy ones, I saw clearly
what mattered.

In the process of living, difficulties had sometimes seemed very
important. Too often I had wasted my energy and my attention on
petty annoyances, on the imperfections in life or in myself, on obsess-

ing over painful times. Now I see that what I really value are the good times, the moments of gladness, visions of beauty, and realizations of the perfection of it all. The happy times are what I remember and cherish. Only so many hours, limited in any life. How will they be spent? I find that I do not want to expend them in strife. I want the joy.

I believe now that my existence has a purpose. I thought before the fall that my life was at best randomly donated, at worst a mistake or perhaps even a punishment. Now I feel my lifetime to be given purposefully, not by chance, but deliberately, determinedly, specifically offered back to me from a place of likely death.

Without divine and human intervention, It would have been so easy for my life to simply slip away. I marvel at the interplay of fate and fortune that wove together the miracle of my salvation. What if Jake, Leslie, and Walter had cancelled their trip? Suppose I had not been calling out just as they hiked by? If they had been a day or two later? Or if I had been farther up the ravine, out of earshot? What if Walter had been unable to run? If there had been nobody at Crown Valley? What if the vacationing firefighters had been unwilling to help? Suppose the helicopter pilots had decided not to fly through the dusk? The possibilities go on and on. If any single one of these things had not been in place, I would not be alive now.

I see purpose behind the amazing complexity of the sequence that resulted in my deliverance. That mine is a specific life, given back to me for a definite reason, I now have no doubt.

For the first time in my recollection, I feel that I belong here, on this planet. I feel welcomed by the earth, by the people upon it, by whatever powers conspired to help me. Certain now of the essential goodness of humankind, I believe also in the benevolence of the universe. Surely a world that would provide help to one such as I is a good place in which to live, and just as definitely, the people who surround me are ones that I want to share this world with.

More universally, I feel my own story to be symbolic of all of the hope that exists in the world. The people who helped me to represent the higher selves of all mankind. I believe this to be a world in which despair can be replaced by hope, in which destruction can bring about renewal, in which help can be found, in which good can triumph.

I have had the chance to face my darkest fear, and to find it unfounded. Always a productive sort, blessed by strength, a good mind, a drive to organize and do and help, I had come to feel that these qualities defined my worth, and hence my ability to be loved. Although I had many friends, I was convinced that if ever I found myself stripped of my health, my physical well-being, my capable strength, my ability to take care of myself, my financial solvency, my mobility, I would be worthless and hence alone. I would be unnoticed, unassisted, and most especially, unloved. So assured was I of this conclusion, so much did it define my reality that I never even wondered if there might be another outcome.

The portion of love that I allotted myself was indisputably conditional. My requirements were harsh. I demanded much of myself so that I could deserve what I wanted most. The price I had put on love was that of my own adequacy. Loss of capability, with the resulting loss of love, was my darkest fear.

In the aftermath of the fall, stripped of everything that I felt gave me value in this world, I had the exquisite opportunity to see the lie in that fear. In my darkest hours, so helpless that I could not care for myself, could not stand up, could not pay my bills, and could not even ask for what I needed, my friends, family and community rallied around me and did everything. There can be no doubt in my mind of the love that inspired this collective saving of a life and of a soul.

How many of us have the chance to face our darkest fears, to survive them, and to realize that they are simply not so? If the model that had previously described to me my own value and limited my understanding of self-worth could have been so wrong, what other realities might also be called into question? Which other fears may be unfounded?

With a lessening of fear comes a greater freedom to engage fully with life. I am incredibly blessed to have seen the worst, faced my fear, and lived to know it for the lie that it was.

I know now that I am loved. Even on the worst of days, I remember the people who were there for me in my time of need. They are still there. When I think of it, I telephone a few of them, and tell them I love them.

Previously a capable person, strong, able, I gave liberally of my time and energy and resources to my friends. I sometimes waffled about whether or not to accept offers of assistance in return; often I simply turned them down. Heaven forbid that one should appear needy. Certainly it has sometimes seemed easier to rely upon myself. I know I won't let myself down. Then in one swift step, I was rendered so helpless that the choice was no longer mine. I had to learn to accept help.

I have also learned to allow people the privilege of giving. Had I previously denied others the right to reciprocate, hanging stubbornly onto my own wish to maintain self-sufficiency? Had I been selfish in needing always to give, and not let others give back? In the aftermath of my accident, I saw that people found a sense of purpose in the ways that they were able to help. Some thanked me for letting them be of aid. My need was a blessing to those who wanted to help, allowing them the honor of being of service. I understand now that their desire to give is not meant to diminish me, that their ability to make a difference for someone else has contributed also to their own lives. I am grateful for the help, no longer so reluctant to admit weakness.

For years I'd been chasing a better me. I'd taken seminars and courses, done journalings, visionings, rituals, listened to feedback, adjusted those qualities that could be refined, searched out new ways of being, adopted meditation, tried coaching and counseling, taken self-growth workshops and classes, read books, searched for the new improved Amy. I was always looking for myself just around the next corner.

One quick slam into a bed of rock has brought me home to myself as years of seeking had not done. I know now who I am. I am here, I am real, I am alive. I am who I am. I am the woman who survived that very genuine experience in the ravine. There is no longer any need to look for myself somewhere other than where I am. I recognize myself at last.

The irrefutable intensity of my adventure has put a different perspective on the ups and downs of daily life. I have less of the impulse to imagine conflicts or to magnify the existing challenges of an ordinary day, to create drama. I have a new high-water mark. Rush hour traffic? Missed that plane? None of these things are even close to the worst I have ever experienced. The most difficult of days is minor in comparison to the day when I crashed to the rock.

I appreciate each step I take on my newly healed limbs. I know just how close I came to not having the use of them, and I cherish each motion, each pace, each scamper. I can no longer abuse my body, driving it to exhaustion, or cramming it stationary into one position for long hours. My once-broken legs squeal in protest, and I must acknowledge my body, and care for it, moving, stretching, and resting.

I believe myself to be less in charge of my life than I had previously thought. I do not acknowledge that I created that step. I did not want to break both of my legs. I do believe that it was meant to be, that some power, greater than the simple creations of my own imaginings, had determined that this was a necessary part of my path. Perhaps there was simply no other way to subordinate my stubborn determination to the demands of the inevitable.

Perhaps it's not about me at all. Could others be meant to vicariously learn these lessons, receive these same gifts, through my story? Maybe I am simply a ripple, my accident meant to influence in ways that I will never know. "Yes," says the little voice in my head, like the peal of a bell in perfect tune.

35

Spiritual Tools for Physical Survival

How had I managed to endure? I often wonder. In many ways, I consider myself a fairly ordinary person. I have a home, a child, jobs and friends, taxes and holidays, just as most of us do. I have the same sorts of problems and joys that punctuate the customary human experience. Why had I survived, given the almost impossible odds? How had I somehow known what to do? What was it about my life that had prepared me to face an ordeal of the magnitude of this one, to hang on until I could be rescued?

My mind flows back over my forty-some years of living. I had pulled wisdom from every aspect of my previous life, bits of knowledge flowing back to me from every resource I had known. Somehow this diverse information wove itself together into a cohesive whole, bringing me the knowledge that was essential to sustain a life. I had been given exactly what I needed to live through this experience.

Of all the information I had gained, of all the gifts I had available to me, the spiritual tools, the intangibles, were what gave me the faith, focus, and hope to physically survive until my miracles could find me.

1. Look, Listen, and Learn

My parents had given me a good start, bequeathing to me their creative spirit and solid determination. I had learned basic first aid in school and at the YMCA: the wisdom of wound cleansing and antibiotic application, the necessity of using pressure to stop excessive bleeding. A casual conversation with a friend told me about blood poisoning. The dangers of excessive tourniqueting were illustrated by a movie. A paragraph in a magazine described the threat of dehydration. News stories about disaster survivors inspired my resolve. Unlikely heroes and heroines were offered up by the books I had read. Real people supplied other examples. I recall the innocent voice of my son, refusing to believe in the impossible. I had my own fund of mountain experience to see me through. I had paid attention to park bulletin boards and newsletters. From working hard, I had come to understand fortitude. I knew what it took to get something done. I had learned from my association with spirit.

I had met many people and encountered a multiplicity of environments and belief systems in the course of my lifetime. I had listened to those I met, read their words, heard their messages, even though I did not always understand.

One often doesn't know what will be useful at some future time, or in what way it will help. I believe that none of the wisdom that flows by us is given by chance, that no convergence is random, no meeting accidental. Many seemingly trivial bits of data came back to help me in my time in the ravine.

All had contributed to the pool of knowledge that became mine, the resource that supported me during my trial. The unifying factor is simple. I had learned from my life.

2. CREATE A WORLD IN WHICH HELP IS AVAILABLE TO THOSE WHO NEED IT

I was sleeping, but somehow sensed the urgency of a faint scuffling sound coming from the bathroom. Looking into the bathtub, I found Snowflake, a partially tamed feral cat that my son and I had adopted. She was panting feebly and foaming blood at the mouth. Usually too wild to approach, she now looked at me trustingly. An emergency vet call and several hundred dollars later, I found myself patiently feeding Snowflake with a syringe through a tube in her neck. This went on for a couple of months, taking many hours of time and much patience. Why I was spending such a ridiculous amount of effort on a small worthless animal? It was a clear choice to me. I simply felt that no living thing that came within my range of influence should go without help. I remember thinking that in some way I was creating a world in which there would be assistance for any who needed it.

Snowflake lay passive in my lap and looked up at me. "You are good," said her limpid gaze.

On another occasion, I was out hiking with Francesca and Matt. Matt had become injured, his hip damaged enough to make walking out an improbability. Supporting him as much as we could, we struggled onward. At dusk, Matt clearly in great pain, and temperatures dropping rapidly, I volunteered to hike up the steep hill to the trailhead to find aid. I later wrote about the experience:

"Today, I had been one of the rescuers. Some other day it might be me who needs help."

I remembered those words a year later when my prophecy came true, when I myself needed care so badly, when Matt made a flyer for the HelpingAmy fund-raiser, and brought homemade pizza and fresh figs to Carla's.

3. KNOW WHAT YOU WANT THE OUTCOME TO BE

I began my scootch down the ravine with one goal in mind. I had absolute certainly. I wanted to live. That was the motivation for all else I did, for every intention I carried with me. Know what you want.

4. NEVER GIVE UP

"Never give up," I told Derek, the reporter from the Santa Rosa Press Democrat, when he asked me what message I would like to pass on from my experience. I did not hesitate in my response. I was in a hospital bed at Carla's, and could not stand, or even pay my bills. I was not going to give up.

Even when lying in the ravine, both legs useless, with no other human beings for miles around and precious little hope for rescue, I did not give up.

5. ACKNOWLEDGE THE INTERPLAY BETWEEN ATTACHMENT AND SURRENDER

I found myself very attached to the outcome of my adventure. I wanted my life. I would not give way. I was determined.

And yet, I knew that everything I could do might still not be enough to save me. There was no way for me to control the ending. I had to surrender to whatever the conclusion might be.

Is the secret to be attached? Or to surrender? They appear to be opposing concepts. I have come to believe that the two are intricately related, not antithetical, as it would seem at first. I had not given up, but I had surrendered.

I wanted my life, wanted it badly, and acted upon that choice. It seems clear that my actions contributed to my being found. Jake would not have heard me if I had been farther up the ravine. It also seems likely that my strong desire to live helped to shape my fate in more esoteric ways.

But there were no guarantees. Even my prayers did not bring the assurance of a particular outcome. Ultimately, my future would not be controlled through some choice of mine. Everything that I could do to help myself might still not be enough. I was forced to relinquish my own sense of power, acknowledging that my fate rested upon the decision of some force greater than my own. I felt myself to be shaping my future in conjunction with the powers that be, in tandem with fate, in cooperation with destiny. I yielded to the uncertainty of my circumstance and gave up my desire to know what would happen. But I never gave up hope.

Would I be OK with whatever should happen to me? I would have to be. It was the only choice I was willing to acknowledge.

Determination cleared the way for even greater surrender. Acceptance made an open space for the clarity of a determined goal; no flotsam and jetsam in the way, no niggling doubts, no room for any uncertainty. Strong desire in its purest form is a beautiful thing. So too is the relinquishment of self that comes with surrender.

And so went the interplay of attachment and surrender, the dance between my own resolve and my admission of powerlessness that shaped my experience and ultimately led to my rescue and restoration. Like the sound and the silence, the melody and then the pause, each concept is defined by the other. The desire and the release play harmony through a life.

Be attached. Be very attached. Know what you want, and go for it wholeheartedly. Then surrender completely to whatever the outcome may be.

6. ALLOW FOR THE UNEXPECTED

In the quality of surrender, in giving in to the unknown, admitting that you may not know the outcome, and may not be able to control it, you allow yourself to experience anything, no matter how unexpected.

When he was ten, my son Sam used to like to watch pro-wrestling on TV.

"What do you see in this stuff?" I would ask, finding the theatrics ludicrous. "You know it's all made up."

"Anything can happen," Sam responded. This is one of his maxims for life. I like to think of these words, for I find great wisdom in them. The words imply acceptance of one of the only certainties of life. Life, by its very nature, is impermanent. The only constant is change.

Expect the unexpected. Your fortunes could change with just one step, and change back again with something as simple as two toots of a whistle. One day you could suddenly be $300,000 in debt, and the next day you could be debt-free.

To think that we know the way that life will play out is to limit the possibilities. Not to know is to invite the impossible, to open to the infinite potential of the unexpected. Allow for something even better than what you can imagine to manifest. Believe in the possibility of miracles. Expect the unexpected.

7. NARROW YOUR FOCUS

The goal of rescue was too unlikely and too distant for my traumatized mind to embrace all at once. I knew what I wanted, but looking too closely at the extent of my desire and the doubtfulness of success would derail me.

As my friend Linda, a home school resource teacher, likes to say, "It's all about chunking." She uses this method to direct her students, counseling them to approach a desired body of knowledge in manageable chunks, learning it piece by piece until they have gotten it all.

Facing overwhelm in the ravine, I would narrow my focus down to smaller and smaller pieces until I got to one that I could handle. Could I think of the next day without being paralyzed by terror? Could

I consider the coming hour, the next ten yards? Perhaps it was only five minutes or a few inches. Whatever it took, I kept condensing my thought until I could manage without confusion, narrowing my task down to a manageable portion, and attacking my goal one bit at a time. Whatever piece I felt I could surround with my mind, I would focus on. Chunk by chunk, I scootched my way down the ravine toward eventual rescue.

8. LOOK FOR THE GOOD

During the year that I had spent engulfed in depression, I had suffered the intense agony of emotional pain from inhabiting a world so filled with misery that it seemed close to unbearable. I suffered so much that I wondered at times if it was worth going on. I would have contemplated suicide, but I was too limp to take decisive action. I was too stubborn, or perhaps too enmeshed in hopelessness to seek help. Friends could see that something was very wrong, but there was little that they could do.

"Train yourself to look at the good things," recommended Carla. I was annoyed. There were no good things. Surely she could see that.

When the numbing misery began to lift slightly, I tried it. This simple device seemed idiotic at first. I made a daily list of what was good. My cat loved me. I had milk for my coffee in the morning. It wasn't raining. It was an impoverished little list, but as time went by, I would use the device whenever I felt the dark claws of depression pulling me into the pit; immediately focusing on something good. I'm going out to get Ben and Jerry's ice cream. I have a new pair of red socks. Look, the sun is shining on a blade of grass. Slowly the device became second nature. Life was still horrible, but I could pull myself out by shifting to thoughts of what was good, no matter how minimal.

In the ravine, I used this same training of attention. I was in a bad situation, undeniably and overwhelmingly horrible. When my mind was foolish enough to touch upon the terror of my plight, I would turn my focus to what was good. The sunlight on the edge of a leaf. The scent of fresh pine needles. The blessings of having my gear with me and a stream nearby. I could not afford to consider the atrocity of my situation, lest I become paralyzed by loss of hope. Despair would kill me as surely as the infections that crept through my body.

9. MAKE A PLAN

My plan was simple. I would work my way down the ravine closer to possible rescue. The plan gave me hope. It gave me focus. It gave me empowerment. There was something I could do to alter my circumstance.

I backed up my master plan with a plan for daily routine. Holding fast to the customary small events that gave structure to each day gave me a sense of continuation, a semblance of normalcy in this unusual situation. Making a cup of coffee. Packing up my pack. Reading a few pages of my book. When turmoil or dismay threatened to take over, there was solace in knowing what to do next. Simply making soup could pull me back into the realm of the ordinary, and hence the possible.

The linear nature of both plans, the master plan and my daily routine, provided focused structure in a confusion of chaotic uncertainty. I didn't know what would ultimately come to pass. But I did know what would happen in the next few minutes if I stuck with my plan.

10. DO EVERYTHING YOU CAN

In March of the year of the fall, I had gone to hike Grand Canyon with my friend Ed Lark. Any hike into this awe-inspiring canyon is an extreme experience. A vertical mile to the canyon floor, and a huge expanse of wilderness with a harsh desert climate, make death by heatstroke or dehydration an imminent possibility. We watched a mandatory preliminary video outlining the dangers and rigors of Canyon hiking and emphasizing the point "You may not be rescued."

We were both seasoned hikers with a healthy respect for the dangers of the Grand Canyon. Each year, hikers die there due to foolishness, negligence, or simple misfortune. We were fit, well-prepared, careful, and lucky. When we completed our grueling, weeklong hike, we were exultant, congratulating ourselves on the magnificence of our trip and the strength of our bodies. At a park bookstore, Ed picked up a book called *Over the Edge: Death in Grand Canyon*. Elated by the successful completion of our mission, we laughed over the book and read chapters to each other on the plane on the way home. Having faced an experience in which death was a possibility, we delighted in life.

Many of the book's stories involved stupidity: blatantly ignoring warning signs, stepping too close to the edge to get that souvenir photo, clowning around, diving into shallow water, or scoffing at the threat of dehydration. Some of the tales were of simple misfortune.

The account that impressed me the most concerned a priest, Father Gavigan, and two teenage boys. They had set out on their ill-advised trip in the middle of a very hot day (it can get to 120 degrees in the shade) with little food and less water. The priest perished in a fall, and one boy died of dehydration just forty-five minutes from the river. What lingered in my mind was the story of the second boy, John Mansfield Owens III, found alive weeks later. He had been as ill-prepared and uneducated as his less fortunate friends, but he had simply refused to give up. Through horrendous days and nights, with precious little information about wilderness survival, he had tried anything, scrawling notes in the sand, building a raft out of driftwood and his belt, making distress signals with sticks and mud, chewing on cactus pulp and mesquite beans. Some things worked and others did not. Finally he was found, through incredible luck and his own persistence. He had done everything he could think of, and some of those things had worked.

This story came back to me as I sat stranded in my ravine. I, too, determined to try everything.

11. COUNT

I used this device several times during my ordeal: when airlifted out, swinging under the helicopter, and while being transported to UMC. I use the same tool often in life. When a task appears impossible, seems without perceivable completion, requires an unknown amount of effort, to simply count brings it back into focus.

I make deals with myself. "I'll hike another hundred steps, and then I'll stop and take five breaths. I'll hike a thousand steps and then I can sit down on a rock. I'll climb three thousand steps before I turn around and look to see how far I've come. I'll write two pages and then I'll have lunch." Often I renegotiate when I reach the end of my deal. I never agree to count endlessly; I focus on a specific number. If I reach that number, I am allowed to choose another.

The device creates a finite ending for a task that seems infinite. It reshapes any goal into a measurable human experience. I can engage in anything for a qualified amount of time.

12. PRAY

Pray to whatever powers of good you acknowledge. Pray to God or to Goddess. Pray to any entity that you feel a relationship with. Pray to your own self.

There is something about the nature of disaster that brings us closer to the veil between the human and the divine. Whatever you believe or don't believe, a time of challenge is an exquisite opportunity to seek help from a higher power or from your own highest self. Miracles are more noticed in times of great intensity. Crisis often brings out miraculous powers in ordinary humans, and touches the angel in each of us. Challenge enables us to access the qualities which are extraordinary, to connect with the divine, within and without.

36

Gratitude

The final tool for survival, in ordinary life and in any extreme situation, is that of gratitude. Gratitude reminds the universe that you appreciate the blessings that come your way. It tells others that this is a world worth living and participating in.

Gratitude is a recognition of the gifts that are offered to us. It opens the way for more of them to pour through, to be acknowledged, and to be spread. It creates a state of grace that plays out past, present and future. What we are grateful for in our past, we acknowledge in our present, and want to extend into the future, for ourselves, and for those around us.

Gratitude creates a disposition that defines a way of life. What we have gratitude for, we also want to bestow on others. A world which serves us well should serve others in a similar way. To live in awareness of the benedictions that come to us is a step in acknowledging a universe in which those sorts of miracles are available to all, and to enlist ourselves in the perpetuation of a world that offers up those blessings.

Gratitude for my salvation inclines me to want to bless other beings in the same ways. About the time that I graduated from physical therapy, our cat Seth was hit by a car. His spine was snapped, and his entire back end paralyzed. Our vet did his best to be realistic about the situation. "It's not likely that he will ever recover."

The echo of his words reminded me of my own situation in the ravine. It hadn't been likely that I would get out alive. And yet I had. I was immensely grateful that I had been given another chance at life. I would offer a new chance to this small cat.

We had his bones set, and got him physical therapy and acupuncture. I spent many hours running micro-currents along his spine, and squeezing his bladder until he regained his own functions. Seth survived, and recovered completely. He is one of the happiest cats I have ever met, perhaps knowing as I know how close he came to not having a life at all. Living in the light of my own gratitude, I never considered that another living thing should not have the same opportunities that I had been given.

Imagine a world in which, for every blessing we accept, we amplify the benefit, and offer it to others, many times over. A smile received is sent back out tenfold. A kind word is multiplied and passed along. A person whose life has been spared then contributes to the lives of others.

Gratitude is a generous emotion. It is about the acknowledgment of giving and receiving, about sharing, a benevolent disposition that does not encourage miserly ways or feelings. Gratitude creates a charity of spirit that is difficult to contain. Though I am individually grateful to each person who helped me, my appreciation for life is not limited in allegiance to any one particular source. My thankfulness surpasses defined boundaries.

"May I say a prayer for you?" said a kindly looking dark-haired woman who had approached my wheelchair. I was outside the hospital, during one of those rare hours when I had been released under my own recognizance to wheel about the grounds. I nodded my accord. One could never have too many prayers.

She placed her hand on my head and murmured a long incantation over me. I did not understand much of what she said, as it was mostly in Spanish, but I could feel that her intentions were good.

She finished her prayer, and I thanked her and went back to my room. The lady followed me. "You know that your being saved is a miracle," she said. I smiled my agreement and understanding. I was still very close to the miracle that was my life, suddenly returned to me. There could be no doubt of my gratitude.

"And now you are going to pray to our lord and savior, Jesus Christ, for your salvation," she said firmly. I laughed.

"No, I'm going to thank the compassion of the great Buddha," I said. "For it was three of his followers who rescued me." Smiling and nodding, she backed hastily out of the room.

What I told her was the truth, but only the partial truth. I am grateful to the Buddha, and to my Buddhist rescuers. But I cannot limit my thankfulness. I thank whichever angels watched over me in that ravine, whatever ancestral ghosts and spirit guides and Gods and Goddesses may have helped. I thank all of the angels in human form who were guided or inspired to find and assist me. I am awash with appreciation for my doctors, for the hospital staff, and for my many friends. I'm grateful to that kind lady for her prayers, and certainly to Jesus Christ as well.

I know so much gratitude that it cannot be contained, ascribed, or limited to any single part of the intricate design that resulted in my restoration. How can I assign my appreciation of the immense blessing of life to just one form, one deity, to even just one miracle? To do so seems like sacrilege. I would be denying all else that I am grateful for, and there is so much. How can I be thankful for life without acknowledging it, in all of its complex and magnificent totality?

I think of how grateful I am, and my heart swells to bursting, expanding so that it pushes the boundaries of my body outwards into the vastness of the universe, and I know no limits of space and time. I can still hardly fathom how it all came to be. I am indebted to all existence.

I look at the perfection of my journey, at the amazing intricacy of the individual parts, formed together so perfectly into the whole that is me, alive and well, restored to all that was lost to me, and I am filled with wonder. And with gratitude.

37

Back to the Mountains

It is May of 2005, one year and nine months since the fall. I have a few days off, so I pack up my gear and head out.

My friends have gone back to their lives, and I have resumed my own. Carla is taking care of her aging father. Adrian is busy with a new girlfriend. Sam has turned eighteen, and is refurbishing his car, a 1965 Pontiac GTO. I'm soloing again.

I love the feel of the open road. The miles flow by, easy as footsteps, one after the next. Intending to go to Henry W. Coe Park, my favorite spring backpacking site, I notice I have passed my turnoff. I'm heading south on Route 99, toward California 180 East. So that's where I'm going. Kings Canyon National Park. I want to see my mountains.

I park myself in a cheap hotel in Fresno for the night. Dipping my travel-weary body into the hotel pool, I critique my mangled, bikini-clad form, and find it sadly lacking. As I take a few tentative steps through the chlorinated water, I am suddenly captivated by a sound overhead. I know that sound. Looking up, I am transfixed by the sight of a CHP helicopter flying above me. Following its path with my eyes, I wonder: is it headed for UMC? Is it taking someone to the ER? Is it the same helicopter that carried me to safety? For a moment, I am back in time, feeling myself dangling below the blue and white copter, recalling the vibration of the whirling blades, reliving my terror. I remember the agonizing pain and the sense of relief when we landed on the hospital rooftop.

Then the helicopter is gone. I look down at my brilliant teal bikini with tropical flowers printed all over and smile at the colors. I stretch out my arms and plunge headfirst into the delight of the cooling waters, loving the feel of my body in motion. I do a few laps, just because I can. Life is good.

Next morning, I head up 180 toward the mountains. My mountains. I gaze upwards past foothills to the Sierra looming beyond. Rays of sunlight reach through scattered clouds like the fingers of God, stretching down and touching the peaks. I climb still higher in my car, entering Sequoia/Kings Canyon National Parks. Taking the turnoff, I pass Grant Grove, following the Scenic Byway as it cuts deep into the heart of magnificent Kings Canyon, following South Fork Kings River toward Cedar Grove.

Something akin to fear clenches in my gut; the panic of the unknown or the terror of remembered falling, I don't know what sort of fear. A spreading heat ignites my lower belly, adrenaline coursing through my body like mountain blood. I know this feeling now. There is fear here, but excitement too. The mountains are calling me. As if longing for a lover's caress, I yearn for the touch of the wilderness. Yet I am afraid. I feel tentative and shy, a woman approaching a long-lost love. Am I still wanted? Will I still be welcome?

I continue down to Cedar Grove and past it, to Roads End. Roads End, the place where my trip began, that incredible journey that almost meant the end of my life.

There is no ranger in the hut at the trailhead today. It is early in the season. The high country is still buried deep in snow, but a message board tells me that the Bubbs Creek Trail is open as far as Lower and Upper Paradise Valley. That's where I'll go then. To Paradise, along the same route that I had taken at the beginning of the trip that led me to that fateful fall. I self-register, getting my permit for the nineteen-mile round trip.

After driving back to Cedar Grove, I call Carla from the pay phone.

"Guess where I am!" I know she'll want to hear about my big adventure. "I'm fine," I add hastily, thinking I hear fear in her voice, and remembering that other phone call.

I tell her where I'm calling from, what my plans are, when I'll be back. She asks questions about my location and projected itinerary. I can tell she's writing down the information. "Send someone to find me if I'm not back in four days," I tell her. As if I had to.

I park my car in the same spot where I had parked it almost two years ago. I am still trepidacious. Will new fear diminish the pleasure I take in these mountains? Will I still love what I once loved the most? I have to find out. I swing my trusty GoLite pack onto my back.

Hiking up the trail from Roads End, my legs hurt a bit. Will my body function adequately? Will my legs be durable enough? After all these months, they are still recovering their strength. Even this moderate trail will be challenging. Will I fall again, perhaps this time not to be so lucky? Will I be OK? Will I make it?

Many things are reassuringly the same. I have much of the same gear.

A few things are different. A new trekking pole replaces the one left in the ravine. I've added a cushy inflatable Therm-a-Rest, pad to cushion my once-broken bones from the cold ground. After eyeing the snow still visible on the peaks, I've traded in my insulated vest for a full-on down jacket. It looks like rain, so I include rain gear as well. I have Jake's whistle safe in my pocket, a talisman against disaster.

I make a mental note to myself to look into getting a 406 MHz PLB (Personal Locator Beacon) before I undertake any longer trips. It would enable me to signal for emergency help via satellite from anywhere on the planet. PLBs have been authorized in the United States since July 2003, a month before my fall. I figure I owe it to the people who love me, and to myself, to increase my chances of coming back safe.

I turn my attention away from my anxiety, and toward the wilderness. Torrential swirls of water roar their approval as they tumble down Woods Creek. A gentle breeze caresses my face. Fear is soon forgotten in the wash of ecstasy that consumes me; senses claimed by newly remembered wonders. I hear the familiar crunch of granite gravel under my boots, the sweet twittering of small birds from the forest canopy above. A million pine needles release their scent, and my nostrils flare with recognition. The heat of my own sweat mingles with the forest odors, and rises around me in comforting reassurance. I gape at the tumbles of huge boulders, taller than men, hurled down the fierce slopes like so many pebbles, as if by the hand of a giant.

Roaring water rushes down the riverbed and over Mist Falls, tossing bleached tree trunks into huge piles, as though they were as light as toothpicks. I marvel at this evidence of the power of nature. This is what makes me who I am. This pure, undiluted connection with the forces of the wilderness speaks to the wildness and power in me. "Remember who you are," whispers the wind in the trees. I start to remember.

My body remembers as well. It does not accede to weakness. It knows itself as strong, and knows the rhythm of that steady trail pace,

Amy in pine needles. Photo by Adrian Morgan.

shoulders, hips and legs swinging easily along, one foot in front of the other.

On past the falls, my trail steepens. Rectangular boulders have been hewn into the shapes of large steps. I gaze up as the glistening white blocks of granite switchback up the mountain face. To me, they look like the stairs to heaven.

My heart expands, bringing a sense of great joy, all but painful in its intensity. The pressure in my chest feels as though my heart is actually growing larger, engorged with the sweet sensation of longing. Like the arms of a lover, my wilderness has ejected me, and now draws me back again.

Six and a half miles later, I camp for the night in Lower Paradise. The place fulfills the promise of its name. There are no other people about, and, this time, no mosquitoes. The river flows gently here, ceasing its tumultuous insistence. The waters are serene and complacent. The land flattens out, park-like, under stately pines. The trees stand like guardian angels, tall and glistening, branches outstretched in silent supplication. Wandering breezes tickle the needles, gentle as the flutter of angel wings, soft as the delicate caress of a beloved. The wilderness welcomes me back.

I've learned some things since I've been gone.

I've learned how volatile life can be. One small step can change a life forever, or even snatch one away. I have learned to hold on tightly to what I've got, to cherish it and appreciate it and love it, because in the flash of a footprint, it could all be gone. I am not as quick to attach permanence to anything I hold dear, but I am more inclined to savor the many joys, to look about me and treasure the golden moments and all of the blessings that I find. I have learned that the things worth living for are the good ones.

I've learned that, even when I go solo, I am not alone. I carry with me memories of the many wonderful people in my life, the awareness that I would be missed if I didn't return, and the certain knowledge of how much I am loved.

I've learned that no matter how bad things seem, they could change in a heartbeat. No situation is so devoid of hope that it elicits despair. Anything can happen. And anything has. Anything could still happen. A miracle might come at any time.

I've learned that there are angels. In the great wilderness of life, any of us could be an angel, a human spark ignited by inspiration or necessity, turning an ordinary mortal into a divine blessing. Any of us could be called at any time to be a miracle for another.

I'm getting that wet-behind-the-eyes feeling that comes only with an incomparable Sierra view or with a particularly poignant thought. I am accustomed, by now, to these spontaneous eruptions of emotion. I think about how much I cherish this moment. Content to see the blessings, I give thanks once again to the powers that be, thanks for this life, for these legs, for whatever wisdom has set me upon this pathway.

A few days later, I arrive safely back at my trailhead, sad that this brief trip has come to an end, but exultant at my victory. I know I will be back.

I can once again climb the mountains that I love. I have my life, my legs, my home, my son, my family, and my friends. I feel welcome in this world, and in this lifetime. I am blessed beyond my ability to comprehend.

Roads End is not the end of the road after all. It is a new start. My story is finished, but rest of my life is just beginning. I can hardly wait to see what new adventures the trail will bring.